MW01122255

Hope
Connections

*Be prepared to be transported through these stories and poems –
from Depression-ridden Edmonton to the jungles of Brazil, an island
in the Philippines to a modern-day home where a mother ponders
the gifting of her prodigal. Well crafted and inspiring, the stories
will capture your imagination and keep you reading to the very end.*

Marcia Laycock
Award Winning Canadian Author and Speaker
https://marcialeelaycock.com/

*The writers featured in Hope Connections managed to not only
delight, move, and inspire me, but they also highlighted the wealth
of talent we have here in Canada. This collection is perfect for those
days you're not sure what you want to read, or don't have a lot of
time for a long book. While the stories and poems are all different
in theme and style, offering a nice surprise each time you start the
next one, they fit and flow well together. This would make an ideal
gift for any reader!*

Ann-Margret Hovsepian
Author and Illustrator
http://www.annhovsepian.com/

*Many years ago, I heard a speaker state that we can live 5 minutes
without air, 3 days without water and 50 days without food but
not one moment without hope. In therapy, providing hope provides
a core essential. This book shares stories and poems depicting chal-
lenging circumstances. Each contains a message of how the Spirit
shines a quiet, gentle, invisible, creative, and uniquely tailored hope
adjusting someone's paradigm towards healing and growth. In our
world of uncertainty and suffering, these messages lighten my soul to
a greater level of gratitude. May they do the same for you.*

Hellmut Noelle
MDiv., M.A. CCC, RCC, CCC-S.
Hellmut was a pastor for over 20 years and is currently a counsellor
specializing in sexual abuse trauma recovery. He is active in his local
church which includes speaking once a month.

Hope Connections

A Collection of Stories and Poems from the Writers' Café

Hope Connections
A Collection of Stories and Poems from the Writers' Café

Copyright © 2020, Writers' Café.

Cover illustration by Connie Mae Inglis

Edited by Will Gabriel

Published by Writers' Café, Edmonton, Canada

ISBN 0-978-1-7772996-0-6

Publication assistance and digital printing in Canada by

PUBLISHING
PageMaster.ca

To all those who seek hope, may you find the greatest hope of all.

May the God of hope fill you with all joy and peace.

– Paul, the apostle

Contents

Introduction

Writers' Café was born May 8, 2013, when five writers arrived at my door.

But that wasn't the beginning of the idea. Late the year before, I had become desperate for like-minded people. I started thinking that surely there must be other Christian writers out there who wanted a place to share their work, where they could feel safe, among friendly encouraging writers. Gradually, I realized that this wasn't just a thought I had come up with on my own. God had nudged me into it. *Start your own writers' group.* The sense became stronger and stronger. But the opposing thoughts were also strong: *I can't be a leader in something I know so little about! How does one structure a group meeting? When? Where? Do I really want one more commitment on my calendar? If I build it, will they come?*

I prayed hard, asking God to show me if this was really an idea from Him. Because there was no way I could do this without Him. I asked for a sign.

A few weeks later the InScribe Christian Writers Fellowship sent its Alberta members a mass email. We need a Christian writers' group in Edmonton. Would anybody be willing to start one?

There was my sign.

Still, I hesitated. But I prayed hard, for three weeks. Out of those prayers, four things became clear. If this venture was going to happen:

1. It needed to be a safe place for writers to come and share themselves and their work.
2. We would meet in the afternoon because my evenings were full enough.

3. The group would meet in my home. A coffee shop or other public place didn't seem to be a "safe" place to share our work.

4. God would direct it.

I replied to the email. Then things moved quickly. InScribe advertised for me. I contacted a few writers I knew. I set a start date. I prayed. And soon I began getting emails. When I was satisfied that they were truly interested, I sent them my address. *Who am I letting into my home?*

When May 8 rolled around, I was nervous. Five strangers showed up, but they looked like pretty decent people. It was obvious from the start that they were as anxious as I was to be around other writers. We immediately clicked. I saw that all of my hesitancy and nervousness had been unnecessary. Hadn't I believed that God had nudged me to start this group? I should have been confident that He would bring the people He wanted and that it would be a safe place from the very beginning. I remember very clearly that most people were anxious to leave that day, but that was because the weather had turned nasty and they wanted to get home before the worst of it hit. It had nothing to do with my home, my hosting, or the other people there.

Amazingly, they came back the next month, and before we broke up for the summer we had decided on a name, based on what people were looking for in a writing group: **C**ommunity, **A**ccountability, **F**eedback, **E**ncouragement = **CAFÉ**. We became Writers' Café.

In September, when we started up again, a few more joined. Over the years, others have come along. Some tested the waters for a short time and didn't stay, but the core people have been around from the beginning. At present we have eight committed members who come every month. One of our members travels two hours, one way, to be with us.

We range from beginning writer to published author; cover genres from children's books and stories to poetry, fiction, non-fiction, articles, essays, memoir, and blogging. Each writer is on his or her own writing journey. Each voice is unique. But we all come together in unity and mutual respect.

I discovered I really didn't need to worry about leading. I host and facilitate, but we all learn from each other. We have become bonded, and the trust we have established is of inestimable worth. God is present. It is His group, after all. Together, He is molding us and making us into the writers He wants us to be so that we will use our gifts in our unique ways to bring Him glory, make Him known, and sometimes just delight Him.

Writers' Café now meets twice a month. There is no set agenda. But because I'm a list-maker/scheduler/rule-follower, as each meeting approaches I feel like I haven't planned enough. Then I remember Point #4: God would direct it. From the beginning, God made it clear to me that this safe place needed to remain open to His leading and prompting.

The first meeting of the month includes a short devotional, written by one of our members or not, and a writing prompt. Other than that, God directs the topics of conversation. The second meeting of the month is something we like to call Feedback Friday. This is the day we come with work to share, expecting good solid feedback. This is a safe place to share and a safe place to receive critique.

I love Writers' Café, individually and as a group. I have ventured places in my writing that I never would have dared without their encouragement. And their prayers have moved mountains in personal lives too.

This book, *Hope Connections*, is a new venture for us, and a long time in the making. We hope you will read the stories and poems within and come away feeling a little lighter in your journey.

Joy Bailey

Edith Gladstone Takes Note

Bobbi Junior

I know you're wondering why a cultured woman like myself is standing here in the slush and sleet, holding an umbrella in one hand and a notepad in the other.

It comes down to money, plain and simple. I know we women have come a long way since getting the vote, but the man is still expected to bring home the bacon.

Expectations aren't going to put food on the table, though, not when my man is but a shadow of who he used to be. Expectations aren't going to motivate a man who's lost hope.

I can't be worried about hope, though. My goal is survival, and survival is all about money, isn't it?

At first, I did hope. Hoped and waited. Waited and hoped, that he'd get out and look for work. Even then, I didn't just sit around. That's not my nature. I tried to be creative and look for ways to add to our family coffers. Once, I took an old bed sheet, so thin you could see through the middle of it. The edges were good, though, so I cut off the sides, trimmed them into squares, and hand-stitched tidy little seams to make men's handker-chiefs. Took them down to the market there on 97th Street, but they only brought a few pennies. Don't know why I even both-ered. And, oh, trying to hand-sew when there's next to no light . . . Lots of homes have electricity in this modern age, but not ours. Oil lamp and tallow candles; that's how we make do.

Our house, if you want to call it that, has just three rooms for the four of us. We had indoor plumbing on the farm, but not here. Wood stove, a pump at the sink, and a privy by the back lane don't allow for bragging rights. Primitive is what it is.

And that's where my man sits, in a vermin-chewed settee by the window, the only window left with the pane bare. The rest are covered over now, as winter's about begun. Getting wood to seal them in, well that's a story in itself. My son, Eugene—he's 14 now—Eugene found some boards that fell off a train running along the tracks to the High Level Bridge and came up with his clever plan.

But do you know—I caught my boy planning to ride that train's cowcatcher downtown one day? I put a stop to that, you can be sure. Doesn't matter how slow that engine creeps along. If he were to fall, well, "There's no money for a doctor to stitch you up," I told him, "so just you keep your feet on the ground."

Lynn J. Simpson

*"Lots of homes have electricity in this modern age, but not ours.
Oil lamp and tallow candles; that's how we make do."*

But he did see those boards spilled along the track and together we gathered enough to cover all but the one window.

Eugene found some bent nails down where they're constructing that new school near Mill Creek Ravine and straightened them out, pounding them against the railway track. He's a strong, stocky lad, and handy with a hammer, is Eugene. Covering the windows and figuring out how to do it was his idea, so he redeemed himself a bit after the cowcatcher fiasco. There's very little light reaching into the shack now, but the cutting crosswind is much reduced. I'm going to count that a blessing.

It was the slaughter of our herd that pushed my man over, you see. Bovine tuberculosis they called it. We'd worked over a decade to build that herd out there north of St. Albert. Then the vet came one day and, well, you just never know, do you?

After that, try as we might, Duncan and I couldn't get the farm back up and running. When the bank foreclosed, we moved here to Edmonton, just in time to become a statistic in this God-forsaken depression Mr. Frank Oliver writes about in the *Edmonton Bulletin*. All across the continent, he says it is, and no end in sight.

I wonder to my man, "Is it going to last until we're dead in the grave?" He just stares at me, his eyes already dead it seems.

When the cows were found with TB and all of them had to be slaughtered, it was as though his heart was slaughtered right along with them. Everything we'd worked to build oozed into the ground with the blood of those animals. Duncan might as well have stood under the knife and had his throat slit right along with them for all he's been worth ever since.

So you see, I had no choice but to drag my children and my man here to Edmonton. Don't know where we'd have been had my father not left me that shack up from the train tracks. Mind you, it wasn't even fit for squatters when we arrived. All those hobos trekking from Calgary to Edmonton, riding the CP freight trains, you'd think some would have taken up residence in that hovel of my father's, but no. Even the tramps thumbed their noses at it.

But there we are. Four of us who used to live in the most beautiful yellow farmhouse—a veranda wrapping three sides around, and on the table fresh cream and eggs every day, meat from the cattle, and our own grown vegetables. Now we have broken slabs of brown lino covering a dirt floor in three dark rooms cut through with the wind, and pots under the leaks when it rains.

I'm finding ways, though, and I'm teaching my girl. She's almost 12. Cecile is her name. Thin and gangly, with fine, straight hair the colour of a parsnip, poor thing. And she squints. I'm sure she needs glasses, but now's not the time.

When we first came to Edmonton, I had no clue how we'd survive. We're God-fearing people and we soon found Knox Church, just over here off Whyte Avenue.

Walking distance, you know. Very community-minded they are. They'd posted an announcement on the church board telling people how to get on the dole. I have to be honest; I memorized the information so no one would see me writing it down. That's a humiliation I never could have outlived, I can tell you. Really, my soul couldn't have borne it.

It was Cecile I'd send off to the grocers with the food vouchers they handed out. I certainly wasn't going to show my face with that in hand, to be marked by the neighbours with the shame of government assistance.

One day, I remember, the girl took a dreadfully long time getting home with the canned corn beef and potatoes I was waiting on to make our supper. I asked her what took so long, and she said she was waiting by the bus stop until no one else was in the store. I didn't think about it at the time. Refused to, if I'm honest. Sometimes, now, I do think about it. Maybe it was wrong of me to expect the girl to bear humiliation I couldn't bear myself. Maybe. I don't dwell on it though. That's all water under the bridge.

And there's different kinds of water under different kinds of bridges, believe you me!

Every month the girl and I, we walk across the High Level Bridge to the YWCA there on 103rd Street. Now I admit, I might glance over the rail of that bridge sometimes, but I don't pause. Not ever. I've seen those that pause—those that stop and look down into that bleak, black water. It's as though it's calling them and they can't resist. Terrible for their families, just terrible. Somebody once said about those tempted to succumb to the dark-water call that we must not use our freedom to violate our freedom. I don't exactly know what that means, but I do know I won't take that route. I won't so much as consider it. No one can say Edith Gladstone gave up, and I won't let the girl give up either. We keep walking across that bridge with our heads high because we have a destination, even if it is just the YWCA and their monthly clothes drive.

We have a technique, Cecile and I. Pretty clever, if I do say so myself. We look for the shabby garments, threadbare with holes worn through, and they let us take a bag full for just two bits. At home we sort out the ones that are similar in colour. It's easy to find browns and greys, but Cecile makes a point of searching for reds and blues. She likes the bright colours. Then we cut out enough decent material to piece together something to clothe ourselves—a skirt, a vest, a cape. We're making patch-work clothing the latest fashion, don't you know! I thank the good Lord we didn't sell the treadle sewing machine when we left the farm. Duncan wanted to, but I was adamant. I knew we'd need it, and I was right.

We did use our pennies to buy a proper second-hand suit for Duncan, though.

Soap too. If any man is going to get a job, he has to look and smell like a gentleman. So there my man sits, day after day, clean smelling and tidily dressed in his dark brown, knees-shiny suit, doing nothing. Nothing at all.

Oh, do you smell that? They're baking fresh buns in the diner here behind us.

Standing in this slushy, windy doorway, it's like my nostrils are taking off on their own journey, savouring that delicious aroma. I just wish they wouldn't leave my belly behind. Expecting the smell of that bread to fill my gut is as futile as trying to get my man up and moving.

Now, I know that to some folk, women working a job is offensive. They say our place is in the home and it's men who should be the breadwinners, but my man isn't winning anything, let alone bread, so I have no choice. And that's what I'm doing in this doorway, truth be told. I'm here on assignment from Mr. Frank Oliver, publisher of the *Edmonton Bulletin*, don't you know.

Mrs. Morris Hapford is the president of the South Side Ladies Benevolent Society. Those good ladies meet in the side room of this diner every month. With the permission of Mrs. Hapford, Mr. Frank Oliver is paying me to sit in on their meeting and record all the fine things they're doing for the poor here on the South Side. There're twelve in the society, so I'll be sitting in the thirteenth chair. I'd rather it were the fourteenth. I'm not superstitious mind you—it's just that an even number is more orderly is all. And fourteen halved is seven, and isn't that the Lord's number?

But I'll take the thirteenth seat as bidden. I'll be quiet as a pebble of course. I know my place. I'll just be a pair of ears, making my notes as I listen to them discuss the plight of the poor—making their plans with the confidence that comes from a soft-bed sleep and a full-belly breakfast.

Do you know how I came to have this job? It's remarkable, really. Unbeknownst to me, Mr. Frank Oliver was standing behind me at this very eatery a few months ago. I was standing just inside the door enjoying the lovely aromas when the proprietor eyed my frayed cuffs and collar and suggested I move on, just as snooty as could be.

I wasn't going to take that, so I turned the tables on him and pointed out several grammatical errors on the menu posted at the door. He huffed at me and I huffed back. I turned to leave, and that's when I ran smack into Mr. Frank Oliver. I recognized his majestic flowing moustache from his picture in the paper. He was very polite and apologized for bumping into me, and I apologized in turn.

But then he asked me where I was educated. When he heard I'd been tutored in London, England, well, his eyes lit right up and he asked if I'd be willing to sit in on the various ladies' meetings in the community and take notes. Would I be willing! He said the *Edmonton Journal* was running columns about the Edmonton Society, and he needed to have something comparable in the *Bulletin*.

That uppity *Journal* is a Conservative rag, don't you know? They'd never hire a woman. I've heard stories of their old boys' club, believe you me. That Southam family that owns the *Journal* has always pandered to those supercilious political gents. But Mr. Oliver is a Liberal and a forward thinker. Mr. Frank Oliver believes in hiring women, and the woman he hired is me!

Who would have thought that my parents sending me to stay with my dry old auntie in London for my last year of schooling would some day allow me to earn enough to keep the wolf from the door?

Oh! Do you smell that? The eatery's preparing for the midday meal now. They're searing meat to add to the soup—beef by the smell of it—and it'll simmer until noon. It's enough to make your innards chew on their own selves when a body's so hungry and there's naught in the icebox at home. Not that we could afford any ice, even if we did have a bit of gristle to keep cold.

I won't dwell on that though. I'm here to do a job. Mr. Frank Oliver values my skills as a listener, an observer, and a writer. How did he put it?

I have been assigned to note what goes on in the meeting

and write about it in order to inform the good citizens of Edmonton as to the benevolent activities of genteel ladies such as Mrs. Morris Hapford. Mr. Frank Oliver says he considered having a man do this society-reporting job, but he believes that no man can hear women's words through a woman's ears. And that's why the job was offered to me.

My mother, God rest her soul, would die of apoplexy if she knew her daughter was working for a wage, but I have to feed my children, and I'll do what it takes because there's no one else lining up to take on the task.

Yes, it's been hard. Yes, we're still struggling. But here I am with a job. A job! Waiting to go in and sit in the thirteenth chair and listen as these ladies have their South Side Benevolent Society meeting.

In a different time, a different place, I would have sat with them as a peer. I wouldn't be waiting to fill my notebook with pencilled scribbles about their community-minded activities.

In a different time, a different place—but no. Here I am. In this time, in this place.

And you know, I have a coat, I have shoes, and I have a job. We're not on the dole any longer, and we'll have a meal when I get home. Meagre maybe, but a meal nonetheless. The wood stove gives us heat. The pump gives us water. My children are going to Rutherford School, and they're clothed—maybe not fashionable, but clean and warm.

And my man, if he ever starts to stir again, will have clothes to wear to look for employment when he's ready one day.

One day.

Ah, there's Mrs. Morris Hapford, ready to open the door for the meeting, so I'll be on my way. For now, it's this day. This is the only day I need to manage, and this day I'll manage just fine.

Prodigy
(1996)

Joy Bailey

Taryn is up early. Again. So I've missed out on the two hours of sleep I desperately needed after dealing with a teething baby all night.

Once Taryn is up, the whole household is up. We have tried to explain to her that she mustn't disturb us so early in the morning.

She tries. I know she really tries, but she can't keep herself away from that instrument and the music welling up inside her. Every waking moment that she's not eating or doing school-work, she's at the piano. Sometimes I even have to remind her to use the bathroom.

Her schoolteacher tells us she is a good student. But when-ever her hands are not occupied, her fingers move soundlessly through the air as she plays the mysterious music in her head.

It's not just that she plays anything she hears. At least, not anymore. These days, she's exploring. Experimenting. Lately her improvisations have become . . . unnerving. The manipulating of well-known popular or classical tunes, the variations she comes up with on the spot, the going over, and over, and over— single notes, whole phrases, complete movements. Changing from major to minor, from sweet and melodious to haunting and discordant.

Every day I wonder what "normal" nine-year-olds are

like. What are their households doing at five a.m., ten fifteen, bedtime? Are their lives bombarded with rhythmic dissonant crashes, five-minute-long trills in the highest register, or a single note played 831 different ways over a stretch of two hours?

I don't want to tether her. She is gifted and must be allowed to create. But sometimes it's at the expense of her family's sanity. Especially her mother's.

Marilyn, her accomplished and caring piano teacher, assures me that Taryn is growing in her ability and encourages me to keep on keeping on. It's been a heavy burden at times to try to decide what is best for her. As a former music teacher, I know music. But I'm out of my depth with Taryn. Several music specialists have shown interest in working with her, but that would

Lynn J. Simpson

"Descending octaves in the left hand temper magnificent regal chords in the right."

mean moving, and Mitchell can't leave his job right now. There is certainly no way we would send her off by herself.

As I lie in bed, eyes closed but definitely awake, Taryn plunges into "O Canada." Descending octaves in the left hand temper magnificent regal chords in the right. Beside me, Mitchell turns over. He stretches and yawns, then drapes his arm around my middle and kisses my ear.

"This little family loves you, Lisa," he mumbles while he nuzzles my neck. "Stay in bed. I'll get breakfast going."

As he plods to our attached bathroom, Taryn begins to expertly play "Kiss from a Rose" by Seal and then transitions into Alanis Morissette's "You Oughta Know," and I wonder if letting her watch the Grammys two nights ago was an intelligent idea.

Suddenly, six-year-old Julia stumbles through our bedroom door, wearing her fairy princess dress and carrying a groggy, runny-nosed one-year-old. He begins to slip out of her skinny arms, and I leap out of bed to rescue him.

"Sweetie! Ben is very heavy for you. Why are you carrying him?"

"I went in hith room and I thaid, 'Ben are you awake?' and he opened hith eyeth and thaid, 'Ba'. That meanth 'take me to Mom,'" she lisps through missing front teeth.

As I plop Ben down on the bed, I try not to envision how in the world this energetic sprite managed to get him out of his crib. I slip my go-to plaid shirt over my tank top and slink my bare feet into my ever-ready boat shoes. Ben looks at me expectantly.

"Ba," he says.

"That meanth I'm hungry," Julia says confidently. She does a twirl on one bare foot and heads out of the room, fairy princess ribbons and tulle wafting behind her.

Taryn is playing Beethoven's "Moonlight Sonata" as Julia, Ben, and I traipse past the living room into the kitchen. I kiss Ben's feverish forehead, put him in his high chair, and give him a few dry Cheerios to keep him happy while I get his breakfast ready. Julia flits around the island, her fairy wings brushing past my legs. Mitchell enters and gives me a questioning, eyebrows-raised look.

Oh right. He was going to make breakfast while I stayed in bed.

I glance at the clock. Three hours til school! I look at Mitchell, tilt my head, and shrug my shoulders.

Just then, Taryn breaks off in the middle of the Moonlight Sonata's hypnotic lull and launches into the thundering military sounds of Chopin's "Polonaise in A major." Ben, who had drifted off to sleep with his face in his Cheerios, startles awake and starts demanding breakfast.

"Ba! Ba! Ba!"

He swipes the Cheerios off his tray.

"Ba! Ba! Ba!"

His appeal becomes less forceful and dissolves into the wails of a teething baby. I pull him from his chair and cuddle him. As I do so, it registers in the recesses of my mind that Taryn is playing the A major Polonaise in C# minor, the same key in which the Moonlight Sonata is written. The ingenuity of it is stunning.

It takes a couple of seconds for my brain to catch up to the moment, but I slowly realize . . . the music has stopped. Ben is sniffling, his head on my shoulder. I pad quietly to the living room doorway, baby on my hip.

Taryn is sitting at the piano completely motionless. Her head is tilted slightly to the right, like it does when she listens to the music in her head. But the astonishing thing is that her hands are not moving. She holds them absolutely still, two inches above the piano keys.

"Mom," she whispers.

She knows I am there.

"Mom, listen!"

I walk over to the piano. Ben lifts his head. His sniffling has stopped.

She looks at me, her eyes wide with wonder.

"Do you hear it?"

I hear nothing.

"It's like . . ." She stops to think of the right words. "It's like, you know, when you blow up a balloon. But then all of that air in the balloon—the quiet—is so big that it bursts the balloon and then the quiet comes down in confetti, all different colours, and it fills every space."

She drops her hands into her lap and leans her head back. Takes a deep breath and smiles. Lets the confetti fall.

I am looking in awe at this gangly, freckled, strawberry blonde. This . . . child.

"Ba?" Ben looks at me.

Julia twirls into the living room and does a tippy-toe dance, ribbon and tulle billowing around her. Immediately, Taryn teases Tchaikovsky's tinkling "Dance of the Sugar Plum Fairies" from the piano's highest register. Both girls laugh. Even Ben begs to go down. He toddles two steps and falls down.

"Hey! Who wants pancakes?" calls Mitchell from the kitchen.

"Yay!" squeals Julia as she skips out of the room. Ben, several feet behind her, crawls on all fours as fast as he can.

Taryn says, "Yes!"

She trots up to Ben, puts him on his feet, takes his hands, and walks penguin-style behind him to the kitchen.

I'm still. Standing by the piano. Taking a deep breath, I let it out slowly. Release my restless thoughts. Lean my head back. And let the confetti fall.

The Traffic Jam

Tina Markeli

Cancer, the dreaded illness,
Snuck into our house recently, but
Concealed its presence until
A short month ago.
Uninvited, unwanted,
It has made itself at home in my body—
A brash houseguest that demands
Our immediate and full attention,
Disrupting our peaceful lives.

I know God is carrying me—but just now
The initial buffer of shock
Has worn out—my brain
Bombarded with information,
My heart assaulted with
Arrows of regret, fear, what-ifs.
How will my beloved cope with
This world of technology
I have navigated on his behalf?

I know that God is going before me,
With me, guarding from behind.
I see it in a thousand details—how
The scheduling of appointments has been so
Uncannily perfect, the information coming
At exactly the right times.
I know God is love, He is good, He cares for me.
But my heart quails in fear of the unknown, fear
Of disgracing Him with my unconscious reactions.

For I know my weaknesses, my failures, my inabilities,
And sometimes the communication highway between
My head and my heart
Becomes clogged with the traffic jam of
Information overload,
Fear of the future,
Fear for my loved ones,
Fear I have done something bad
For this to happen.

But . . .
I know a traffic cop who can step into
The fray of my tangled emotions, clear the snarled
Thoughts, fears, and sense of shame.
Jesus Christ, my friend, my helper, my Saviour,
My advocate.

He tells me to stop
Ask
Listen
Obey
Rejoice
Let His love bring order to the chaos of my mind.

Like a fresh wind, His presence dissipates the fumes
Of fear, worry, anger.
His gentle voice mutes the blaring horns
Of urgent schedules.

My mind is directed to a quiet place,
Peace in the midst of the storm.

Lynn J. Simpson

My mind is directed to a quiet place, Peace in the midst of the storm

Everything I Learned, I Learned from . . .

Connie Mae Inglis

Educating the mind without educating the heart
is no education at all.
–Aristotle

I stretched out on the weather-worn plank bench, resting my sticky back against our nipa-woven house, thankful for siesta time. Our small, four-roomed home sat on stilts like every other house on the island, allowing the air to flow underneath and up through the slatted flooring—a desperate attempt at air-conditioning. I closed my eyes, hoping to catch a bit of that breeze to relieve the oppressive heat—a futile endeavor today.

I thought about the lifestyle my husband and I had chosen in our decision to call this place home—a lifestyle antithetical to the Canadian one we left behind. We came to this obscure island in the southern Philippines with our three young children because we wanted to make a difference in the lives of the Molbog people. To offer literacy classes and basic health and well-being booklets. To offer avenues to pull them out of their poverty. To offer hope. We knew what we were in for, at least in our minds: No roads. No phone. Limited electricity from the solar panels secured to our tin roof. No communication with the outside world except by two-way radio. But we believed this to be our calling and so we came.

Questioning voices of friends and family back in Canada entered my mind:

You're going where? Why? What good can you do for a whole group of poor people?

What a waste of your abilities—your education. Just help the poor here at home.

Lynn J. Simpson

"No roads. No phone. Limited electricity from the solar panels secured to our tin roof. No communication with the outside world except by two-way radio. But we believed this to be our calling and so we came."

You're depriving your children of a good education—and opportunity.

Ah. The comments about our children's education. I had to admit, they did stir doubt in my mind as a mother. Could my children receive a good education out here in the middle of nowhere?

"Mommy."

There it was. The voice of one of my three, putting an end to my reprieve.

"Mommy," my eldest daughter Sarah repeated, her annoyance obvious through the thin walls of the house. "Jesse keeps knocking over my castle."

I returned to my children and our afternoon of home-schooling, blocking out the doubts, fairly content that in using Canadian curriculum I was offering a good education. Yet I was poignantly aware of the contrast outside my walls. Ninety-five per cent of the Molbog children on the island had no formal education, spending much of their day planting or harvesting rice, or washing clothes, or digging for edible roots—anything to help keep their families alive on this unforgiving island. The desire to be out there with the people, offering help in some way, hung like a wet blanket in my mind even as my eldest recited her times tables, as my second daughter practiced her printing, and as my toddler son kept busy with colouring. How does what I am doing at this moment, matter? I couldn't shake the question.

The answer came later that day in an unexpected visitor. Hidden in the shadows of the thatch of our lowered side-porch, I watched through the open window as an unfamiliar woman forced open our slumping, wooden gate, silently ascending the thin bamboo steps to our porch. She cleared her throat to announce her arrival, and both my husband and I stepped down onto the porch to greet her. She looked to be in her forties, though I was not a good judge of age; after the age of thirty, all the women looked older than they were. Customarily shy, she fidgeted with the folds of her faded batik skirt, her dusty bare feet shifting restlessly along the bamboo slat floor. When she skipped the protocol greetings and began her staccato speech, we both knew something was very wrong.

I listened intently, missing much of the detail due to my lack of language study. I only understood that a child had been injured and needed help. My husband, however, had picked up more detail. The little girl had been draped on her mother's back as her mother was working out in the field burning stubble to prepare for the next crop. Somehow the girl had fallen out of the sling and into the hot ash. The woman asked if one of us could come.

"Of course," my husband said, looking at me and mouthing the words, "You go."

"Okay," I mouthed back, yet unsure of how much I could do for this little girl. Then, turning to the woman, I said in broken Molbog, "I will come with you. Is it far?"

The woman turned and pushed out her lips, pointing back to the trail. She offered no further information. Giving my hubby a quick glance of resignation, I scurried up and into the house to grab the medical kit. He followed.

"You can do this, hon," he said, touching my arm. He could always read my mind. "Remember—they don't even know basic health care. Anything you do for this girl will be good."

"You're right," I said quietly.

"Can I come, Mommy?" My perceptive eldest had planted herself noiselessly beside me. Had she noticed the anxiousness in my face?

"That's a good idea," my husband said, looking down and grinning. "You can be Mommy's little helper."

My daughter simply smiled and slipped her hand into mine.

We followed the woman down the trail; she spoke not a word.

"Be careful," I said to Sarah more than once, keeping her hand in mine. I pointed out the dangers along the path: the sharp, camouflaged coral and gnarly palm roots jutting out of the sand; the serrated leaves of the pandan brush that would scratch deep into her soft skin. We soon turned away from following the ocean shore and up into the thicker jungle of the interior.

"Further than I thought," I muttered, looking down at my daughter. "You okay?"

"How old is the girl?" Sarah said, totally ignoring my concern for her.

"I'm not sure," I said, unaware that she had been listening to the conversation back at the house. "Anywhere between two and five is my guess."

"Maybe Jesse's age?"

"I—I guess she might be."

Sarah's questions redirected my thoughts to the non-existent healthcare for the Molbog and their lack of education in simple health practices. They had no understanding of clean drinking water or proper waste disposal. Mothers didn't, or often couldn't, teach their children how to disinfect and bandage even minor cuts to prevent infections so prevalent in the tropics. Neither the parents nor the children had access to immunizations or vitamins or penicillin. Even if they did, there was no money to pay for such luxuries. Then I thought about the quality of life back home. I drank from the tap; I flushed the toilet; I put a Band-Aid on my child's cut. And with serious issues, I relied on the healthcare system—the doctors and nurses and medical centres—with no thought of the overall cost and with little appreciation. It was our right as Canadians. Wasn't it?

But here, in this situation, I was probably the only health care this little girl would ever experience or could afford. Perhaps, I was this family's only hope.

We zigged and zagged to the trail's end, finally arriving at a crude, one-room hut. The woman stopped, turned around at the foot of a set of rickety steps, and jabbered something in Molbog.

Not understanding a word of what she said, I froze. "Help me, God," I whispered. "Help me give hope." I looked down at

Sarah, her wide eyes sharing none of my concern. I squeezed her hand and we climbed the wobbling steps into the unknown.

There, on a low table in the centre of that one room, lay the little girl, a group of adults sitting cross-legged around her, their faces expressing more shame than sadness. I wanted to tell them there was no need for embarrassment—to explain to them my procedure for helping the girl—but I didn't know the words. All I could do was greet each one out of respect and say, "I have come to help." That had to be enough.

I turned to the girl: a malnourished five-year-old. Most of her right side was burned, her thigh and arm the most serious with blistering, second-degree burns. Except for remnants of gray ash, her face was unharmed, for which I was thankful. She looked at me with fearful red eyes; I responded with a slight smile and touched her cheek, forcing down my own feelings of inadequacy. *I have the ability to help this little girl.* I asked for some water, thankful I had remembered those words, and pulled out my soap and bag of clean cotton cloths. I worked slowly and gently, knowing that I was inflicting pain but that preventing infection was the priority. As I carefully wrapped gauze around her thin, delicate foot, leg, and arm, I heard a young voice.

"Mommy?"

So focused on the task was I that I had forgotten about Sarah. She was standing at the end of the table, but in the dimness of the room, I couldn't read her face. "Yes, sweetie?" I said.

"Can I hold her hand? I think I want to."

"Are you sure?" I asked. Realizing I had been casting my own doubts onto my daughter, I said, "Sure, sweetie. You can hold that hand." I pointed to the little girl's left side. "That one isn't hurt."

Without hesitation, Sarah sidled up to the little girl and wrapped her healthy, fair-skinned hand around the thin, dark-skinned smaller one.

I gasped, overcome by the beauty of the moment and my daughter's tender heart. Little did she know that I had been questioning our move to this island—questioning the lack of education she and her siblings might receive. With this one gesture of kindness, she erased my fears, showing me what she'd already been learning in watching my husband and I interact with, and care for, the Molbog people. She reminded me that learning didn't just involve the mind—it also included the heart and the soul.

Would God, or Wouldn't He?

Jack Popjes

Our youngest daughter, Cheryl, was born with amblyopia, commonly called lazy eye—a condition in children when vision does not develop properly in one eye. "Take her in for an eye exam when she is two years old," the ophthalmologist told us "She will need glasses by then." Cheryl was four months old when we left Canada for Brazil for our first term of service as Bible translators.

When she was almost two years old, an epidemic of trachoma swept through the Canela village in Brazil where we worked. This is a serious eye disease that, at that time, had blinded six million people worldwide. Most of the Canela and all our family were infected, and we worked day and night treating the sufferers with hundreds of tubes of Tracomicina, an antibiotic ointment.

When, after a week or so, we changed Cheryl's pus-soaked bandages, we saw that our toddler's lazy eye had turned aside even more. When we returned to Belem, we took her to an optometrist who prescribed glasses and an eye patch to wear over the good eye to force the lazy eye to work. Each year he wrote stronger prescriptions. We were getting increasingly concerned for Cheryl's eye, since there was no improvement, and kept on praying for God to heal her.

Frankly, we were wondering why God hadn't done something for her eye already since it kept getting worse. Besides that, we were badly in need of more financial partners. We were not making it financially and were deeply concerned for Cheryl's eye. Our two-decades-long Bible translation program looked like an unrealizable dream, not a potential reality.

After only three years of service in Brazil, our director came to see us. He praised us for the good start we had made in our work among the Canela. "Your financial support, however, continues to be so low," he said, "that you are borrowing money from other missionaries to buy groceries. You need to go back to Canada and raise adequate support before you return to Brazil."

So, we found ourselves in Calgary in early summer, six months earlier than we had planned. We immediately took Cheryl to an eye specialist. After checking her out thoroughly, he said, "It's a good thing you brought your daughter in for me to examine today. Her prescription is completely wrong; her lazy eye needs a totally different treatment. In another month or two it would have been too late. Even now, we may have to do surgery to keep her lazy eye from going completely blind."

He prescribed different glasses as well as a patch. We kept praying throughout that furlough year. At her last exam he was so pleased with the improvement he cancelled plans for surgery. "In another fifteen years, she may not even need glasses," was his optimistic forecast. During that furlough, many more of our friends promised to support us with their regular gifts and our financial situation also improved.

We returned to Brazil filled with renewed positive expectations that no matter what happened, God would take care of us, our finances and Cheryl's eye. And He did. Eighteen years later, Cheryl graduated from college with near-normal vision. The Canela people had His Word in their own language, and Jesus established His church among a people group that had never known Him.

Lynn J. Simpson

*"We returned to Brazil filled with renewed positive
expectations that no matter what happened, God would
take care of us, our finances and Cheryl's eye.
And He did."*

The Man Under the Street Lamp

Tina Markeli

Patty was ten, old enough to go to Kids Club at the local church by herself and proud to do so. Walking to Kids Club was easy. Even in winter, her anticipation pushed aside any thoughts of danger. But coming home was hard. Would there be a stranger lurking in the dark—a stranger who would hurt her? I suppose in today's world her parents would be considered irresponsible to let a ten-year-old walk four blocks by herself in the evening. But in the 1950s, even in the big city of Vancouver, this was the norm. Patty's parents, immigrants struggling with poverty and her Dad's asthma, were thankful for this safe, no-cost activity for the children of their working-class neighbourhood. Time with friends, lots of fun, and rewards to be earned had Patty and her friends eagerly going back every week.

Going to Club, Patty walked the first two and a half blocks alone to the house of her friend, Gail. The next block and a half felt much shorter: walking with Gail, talking about school, raving about the teachers they liked, and tut-tutting about Miss Trimbath, the stern, old maid librarian that everyone feared. The Red Cross Club was collecting toothbrushes, toothpaste, and soap for hygiene kits for a war-torn country in Africa. Patty and Gail didn't know much about the country, but it made them feel quite grown up to talk about it. Their gold-coloured Kids Club scarves bobbed up and down in time with their steps, showing off the badges they had already earned and inspiring dreams of the badges still to come.

Sometimes they wondered aloud about what they would do when they grew up. They didn't talk about sports. Reading books, learning to crochet, knit, and sew suited their tastes much better. Their goal was to be good homemakers like their mothers. They expected to get married and have children, someday. But that was a long way off. For now, they were busy enjoying their lives. As Patty walked to Kids Club she pushed aside the thoughts of walking home alone.

"Welcome to Kids Club," Pastor Rick's voice boomed, and Patty felt safe. Pastor Rick's voice could whisper like a soft breeze or roar like a lion and made Bible stories come to life. After the story, Dan and Sally, Pastor Rick's helpers, gave each child a worksheet. Patty liked filling in the blanks. That gave her time to think about the lessons. She was good at reading and writing and wrote the answers with confidence. Sometimes she could help others who found spelling more difficult. Helping others made Patty feel good inside.

When the worksheets were done, the children handed them to Dan who marked down points beside their names on a big chart that everyone could see. When you finished ten lessons you would get a badge to sew on your Kids Club scarf. There were also points and badges for memorizing Bible verses, which had to be recited to Sally. Sally made sure that the Bible verses were said exactly right, but in a really hard spot she would mouth the next word to give you a clue. Ten verses earned one badge. Games, learning to tie knots, crafts, or making cookies in the church kitchen wrapped up the evening and earned still more badges. Sally was nice. Dan was nice. Pastor Rick and completed worksheets made her feel comfortable. Kids Club felt safe—not like the dark street outside.

At the end of each school year, Kids Club put on a program for the children to show off their new, sometimes hard-earned knowledge in front of their parents and friends. That was when the badges were awarded. Patty worked hard to earn badges. Each badge was proof of her effort and success, signs of her worth. Each badge added to her confidence and pleasure. She felt special, accepted, and worthwhile. The songs, occasional snacks, and games were all fun. But the badges and the approval of Pastor Rick, Dan, and Sally were even more important to her. All year long she tucked away the knowledge of badges earned, ready to be awarded, as pieces of armour against her fears—especially the fear of the walk home.

For Halloween, Christmas, Valentine's Day, St. Patrick's Day, and Easter they had parties. Bright coloured streamers hung from the ceiling. Curtains sectioned the church basement into secret rooms or dressing rooms for actors. Benches were re-arranged to make room for games. Cakes and cookies appeared. Sometimes Patty asked her Mom to send along cookies, just like the other Moms. Fun and food helped chase away fears, for a time.

Bobbing for apples at Halloween was a bit overwhelming. Patty didn't want to get her clothes and hair wet. Christmas was more fun, with riddles and dress-up clothes and acting out the familiar, beloved Christmas story. For the Valentine's party she counted and re-counted the valentines to be sure she had one for every child in the club, for Dan and Sally, and for Pastor Rick too. She hoped she would get lots of valentines as well, but she knew she wasn't the prettiest or most popular. Making sure that she gave a valentine to everyone would get her at least a "thank you," a bit of recognition from the more popular children.

But no matter how much fun they had, the dreaded moment always came: it was time to go home. She clung to the short reprieve when she and Gail walked together as far as Gail's home. But when Gail went into her house and shut the door, Patty stood alone on the sidewalk; just Patty and the last two and a half long blocks to her own house. In May and June, it was still light, so she didn't mind walking alone too much. But from

Lynn J. Simpson

"Her steps grew slower and slower as she tried to decide what to do. Just two more houses and she would be at the corner and have to cross the street where the stranger stood."

September to April it was dark when she left Kids Club—dark and scary. Would she get home safely?

She recited her Bible verses as she walked as fast as she could. That helped. She sang songs, but under her breath so people couldn't hear her. They might think she was silly. She didn't want people to know that she was scared. Pastor Rick said God knew anyway, so it was okay to pray and tell Him she was scared and ask for help. God would not think her prayer was silly.

One night the fog rolled in, hiding the outlines of houses and trees. She felt even more anxious than usual. As she was nearing her street, something dark took shape under the lamppost on the next corner. It looked like a man. As she got closer, she could see his dark coat and hat. She would have to walk right past him. Who was he? What did he want? Why was he standing there so still?

Her thoughts spun like a top, whirling around and around but not giving her any direction about what to do. Would he hurt her? How could she get past him safely? She thought about going to one of the houses and asking for help. She knew all the families who lived on her own block, the block where the stranger was standing, but she didn't know any of the people on the block where she was walking. Would they help her? Would they turn her away?

Her steps slowed as she tried to decide what to do. Just two more houses and she would be at the corner and would have to cross the street to where the stranger stood. She still couldn't see his face. He stood directly under the street lamp, his hat casting shadows over his face. He looked in her direction. Her heart thumped in her chest and her steps barely moved her body forward. Should she run? His long legs could run much faster than she ever could. If she crossed the street to the left or turned right, he would surely go that way as well.

The stranger spoke. "Patty!" She started running. She knew that voice. This was no stranger; this was her father, come to meet her, waiting in the cold fog that would make his asthma worse, waiting in the dark, watching out for her, ready to walk her home. This stranger she so feared was, in fact, her place of safety and comfort.

Conversations

Bobbi Junior

An Unwelcome Visit

"What in blazes are you doing here, Linda? Just cuz you're my daughter, it doesn't mean you can show up and walk right in my door any old time."

"Well, that's a fine welcome. I'm here because that freakin' homecare nurse has phoned me three times in the past two months to say you cannot live alone anymore."

"She's phoning you? Telling you my business? That's against the law."

"Mom, you put me down as 'next of kin' when homecare started. That means it is my business."

"And just what do you think you and your business are going to do with me?"

"The nurse says you need to put your name down to get into a home. There's a waiting list. You put your name down and then they call you when a spot opens up."

"I am not going into a home. Some stinky place with a bunch of old people shuffling about with walkers? Sitting around, peeing in their pants?"

"You're ninety years old, Mom. You're the freakin' old person. You're already living in a stinky place. It reeks in here. And you've been pushing a walker for years!"

"Well I don't piss in my pants yet, so I don't need no home."

"Man, I come all the way across town to visit you and tell you what the nurse says, and this is how you treat me. You're as stubborn as ever."

"Well, my grandson doesn't think so. He comes to visit me every time him and that little wife of his are in town."

"Trevor visits you because you give him money, Mom. You've always given him money. That's why that son of mine is so flippin' spoiled."

"He's not spoiled. He's a nice boy."

"Well, get Trevor to take care of you, then. I wash my hands of the whole mess. You figure it out."

"I will. I don't need you meddling in my business."

"I'm outta here. And tell that homecare nurse to take me off your 'next of kin' list. When you start pissin' your pants, she can call Trevor. Good-bye."

"Good riddance."

***

Trevor's Invitation

"Seriously, Gran. We'd love to have you come live with us. Jody and I have an extra bedroom in our apartment, so you'd have your own space."

"Ah, Trevor, that's so nice of you. But what would I do out there? Millet's such a little town. And it's an hour away from the city. All my friends live here."

"Yeah, but we go to Edmonton at least once a week for shopping. We could drop you off and then pick you up afterwards. Who's that friend of yours? Irene? You could visit her."

"You'd drop me off? Every week? But what about my stuff? It won't fit into one bedroom."

"We'd put it in a storage locker. They're only, like, $100 a month. We really want you to come, Gran."

"Wait, Trevor. $100 a month to store my stuff? How much would my rent be for the bedroom?"

"Well, what do you pay for your apartment?"

"It's $800 a month. My pension covers it, but there isn't much left for groceries and utilities and things."

"This'll be way better, then. If you give us, uh, say, $500 a month, then you can afford the storage unit and still have some left over."

"Really? Just $500? Trevor, that would be so good."

"It's a plan then. We'll come and get you on the weekend, okay?"

"The weekend? That fast? Are you sure?"

"Sure, I'm sure."

***

Francie and Irene

Sheesh. Who the heck would be phoning me this early? "Hello? Hello? Who's this?"

"Francie, it's me, Irene. Don't yell. Don't you have your hearing aids in?"

"Irene? Why do you always call so early? I'm still in my pyjamas."

"Well I wanted to know what happened yesterday. Did you talk to your grandson?"

"I did. Him and Jody, that's his wife, they want me to come live with them out in Millet. They have an extra bedroom."

"That's so far away. Are you really considering it?"

"Of course I'm considering it. They really want me, and Trevor's such a lovely young man."

"I still think you should let your daughter find you a place in the city."

"Linda was a pain in my butt for years, and now I'm a pain in hers. Serves her right. You'd think at 63 she'd be more mellow, but now she wants to run my life."

"Mother and daughter, like oil and water."

"That's an understatement. But I do get along with Trevor.

Who woulda thought a grandson would want his old gran to come live with him?"

"What about your apartment? What about your stuff?"

"'I'm giving notice today. Trevor's bringing his pick-up this weekend, and they're putting my stuff in a storage place. He's got it all arranged."

"Will you pay rent to Trevor?"

"Just $500 a month. That's for the bedroom and food and utilities and everything. I'll even have money left over. No more scrimping at the end of the month, no more eating mouldy bread."

"Come on, Francie. You know Mildred said the church would give you food hampers when you needed them. You never had to eat mouldy bread."

"I don't need their charity. Mildred and her pastor husband, I know their kind. You take their handouts and they think they own you."

"Well, Francie, I sure hope it works out."

***

Irene Worries

"Hi Mildred. It's Irene."

"Hey, you. How's it going?"

"Oh, good. For me, anyways. I'm wondering, have you heard from Francie?"

"Didn't she go to live with her grandson in Millet? Trevor. Is that his name?"

"Yeah, she did. That was two weeks ago, though, and I haven't heard anything from her. She always calls at least every couple of days."

"Well, maybe she's just settling in. Maybe she's busy doing things with them out there in Millet."

"She's ninety years old, Mildred. She uses a walker. What could she possibly be doing in that little town?"

"Ha-ha! You have a point. Have you talked to Edna? You and Edna and Francie are our three Senior Musketeers. You're always in touch with each other. Maybe Francie called her."

"I talked to Edna yesterday. Not a word. She's been wondering, too."

"Well, why don't you just phone Francie?"

"I don't have her grandson's number and I can't find it listed anywhere."

"Oh. That makes it hard, doesn't it?"

***

Irene Gets a Call

Seven o'clock on a Sunday morning. Who'd be calling me at seven a.m.?

"Hello?"

"Irene? Oh Irene, I got you."

"Francie! Is that you? Why are you whispering? I can barely hear you."

"Wait. I'll go in my room. Now can you hear me?"

"Yes. Are you crying? Francie! Why are you crying?"

"I've tried to call you so many times. They only have this cellular thing of Trevor's. He plugs it in by the TV at night. It's taken me a week to figure the thing out so I could call you. They're still sleeping."

"Francie, what's going on?"

"I gotta get outta here, Irene. I gotta. Every time I turn around, they want more money. Jody needs to pay their heating bill and she's short. Trevor needs money for gas. He wants my debit card, Irene. Says it'd be easier than taking me to the bank every time."

"You can't give him your card!"

"Well, I know that. I'm not stupid. I've been hiding it."

"Oh Francie, don't cry. I'm so sorry this has gone badly."

"Oh, crap. They're getting up. I gotta go."

***

Irene Looks for Help

"I'm so glad I answered Francie's call, Mildred, even though I didn't recognize the number. I mean, it was seven a.m. and I was still half asleep."

"And you say they're asking her for money all the time?"

"Not just asking. She said Trevor wants to take charge of her debit card. Her pension is direct deposit. If he gets her card and PIN number, he can take her money out whenever he wants."

"What do you want to do, Irene? What does Francie want to do?"

"She said she wants to get out of there. Does the church have some way they could help her?"

"I don't know. We have the food hamper program for our seniors, but she needs housing."

"Can't you talk to Pastor? Maybe he has some connections."

"My husband has lots of connections, but I don't think housing old folk is one of them."

"No, I guess not."

"Let me know if she calls again, okay? I'll put her on the prayer chain, too. Maybe God has connections for housing old folk."

"Yeah, maybe."

***

A Second Phone Call

"They're drunk, Irene. Both of them. Passed out drunk. Trevor didn't even move when I took the phone out of his hand. He carries the thing around like some rectangular wart growin' out of his fingers. And did I say they're drunk? Again. With my money!"

"Francie, they don't have your debit card, do they?"

"No. But every time he takes me to the bank, he's trying

to see over my shoulder. I know he's trying to see my PIN. It's real hard to cover it and lean on my walker and hold my purse. Sometimes I get so stressed I put in the wrong number. Then he says I'm a stupid old broad."

"Oh, Francie, I don't know what to do. What can I do?"

"There's nothing to do. I'm trapped."

"But if we could get you here to Edmonton, get your name on a list for a home . . ."

"You still have to pay for a home, Irene. My account's goin' down and down and down. The only thing I can think is to take my walker and go out on the highway at night. There's semis going by all the time."

"Oh, Francie, don't talk like that."

"It's the only solution I can think of. Shoot. Jody's movin'. I gotta go."

***

Irene and Edna Make a Plan

"Edna? It's Irene. Any luck?"

"Yes. I talked to my son this afternoon."

"Dennis, right? He works for Children's Services, doesn't he? What'd he say?"

"He said to call 811. It's a Health Link number for Alberta Health Services. So I called them. I told them what was going on, and that it's elder abuse."

"Elder abuse? But they're not hitting Francie or anything."

"They're stealing her money. She has to sneak to use the phone. She's trapped out there. That's elder abuse."

"Is it? I never thought of it like that."

"Well, anyway, I called 811 and they told me to call something called S.A.G.E."

"What's that?"

"Just a minute. I wrote it down. Here. Seniors Association of Greater Edmonton. S.A.G.E. So I called them. They have a

Seniors Safe House. Can you believe it? There's so much of this they have to set up a house to put the old folk in."

"Can Francie go there?"

"No."

"Why not?"

"She's not independent enough. She needs too much help. But they will arrange for a social worker in Millet to go visit her. If she says she wants to leave, they'll arrange to bring her back to Edmonton, if there's a place she can stay."

"But where's she going to stay?"

"Do you think you could put her up for a bit? I can have her here a few days. And Mildred said her and Pastor could keep her awhile. The social worker will put her name on a list for a home. Then we just have to keep her going until there's an open bed."

"So she'd come here? And sleep with me? But she's a night owl. She prowls all night long. I need my sleep, Edna. I know I'm only 78, but my blood pressure, and my diabetes . . ."

"Just for a few days at a time, Irene. If we all pitch in and keep shuffling her around, I think we could do it."

"And Mildred says she can stay there too?"

"Yes. But her and Pastor don't have a TV. You know Francie won't like being there without a TV."

"She's just going to have to tough it out, then, isn't she? If we're going to do this, she's going to have to give in a bit, too."

"Hah! Francie give in? In what universe?"

"Edna, you're rotten. Okay. If you can arrange for her to be brought back to Edmonton, I'll take her a few days a week. But she has to put her name down for a bed. Before she comes here. That's the only way she can come."

"Agreed. I'll call the social worker in Millet. Grannies to the rescue!"

***

Edna Brings Supplies

"Here you go, Irene. Extra towels, and the shower chair."

"Oh Edna, what would I do without you? I only just remembered that Francie has to have a chair so she can shower. The social worker's bringing her here in about an hour, and you can be sure if I don't have a chair, Francie's going to want to shower right away!"

"And if you do have a chair, she won't want one. Ha-ha! That's our girl!"

"She's lucky we love her."

"She is that. Anyway, the chair's been gathering dust in my basement since Henry passed. I washed it up good, so it's ready to use. Now, Irene, tell me—what did the social worker say? Are they going to charge Trevor? Is Francie going to tell her daughter what's been going on?"

"Not likely. The social worker let me talk to Francie on her phone when they left Millet. Apparently, Francie has to be willing to press charges if the police are going to go after Trevor. Francie said she just wants out of there. In fact, she said if anyone tells Trevor or Jody where she's gone, heaven help them! She acts tough but, really, I think she's terrified of them now. Linda, too. She never did trust her daughter. It's so awful, Edna. They're the only family she has!"

"Not true."

"What's not true?"

"That they're the only family she has. They're not family. We're family. She may be a miserable, cantankerous old coot, but she's our miserable, cantankerous old coot. We've been her family for years, and we'll be her family now."

"For better or worse. I guess you're right!"

***

Sleepless Nights

"Francie, settle down. Can't you just stay still and go to sleep?"

"Where the heck are my glasses? Can't find a flippin' thing in this place."

"Francie. Listen to me! Shoot. You don't have your hearing aids in."

"What? Geez, Irene, you scared the wits outta me. Why aren't you asleep?"

"Why aren't I asleep? Because you're creeping around the bedroom in the dark, banging things and knocking stuff over."

"Wait a minute. You know I can't hear you without my hearing aids."

"Lord, help me. I'm going to kill her."

"There. Now. What did you say? Why can't you sleep?"

"I could sleep if you'd sleep. You can't keep bouncing up and down all night long."

"Well it's not my fault if I have to pee every couple hours. You want me to piss in the bed? Right there beside you? I could do that if you want."

"Oh, shut up. Just . . . Shut up. Go. Go to the living room. Sleep on the couch. Just let me sleep."

"Sleep on the couch? With my bad back? Are you kidding me?"

"I need to sleep Francie. I'm exausted. You've been up every night for the last three nights."

"Well I won't be here come Saturday. I did say I'd go to Mildred's come Saturday. Although what I'll do there I don't know. Can you imagine? No TV. Those Christian folks have some crazy ideas about what's normal."

"I'm Christian. Edna's Christian. And we both have TVs."

"Well, I guess you're abnormal Christians then."

"You might be right. Given what's on TV these days, maybe we are the crazy ones. Speaking of which, you've had my TV so loud the neighbours have been complaining. The apartment manager was by yesterday to tell me to turn it down. If you get me kicked out of here . . .”

“Oh, you’re so smug. Just cuz you have a home and I don’t. Ninety years old and I’m couch surfing. Couch surfing! Me and my walker and my bifocals and my hearing aids and my dentures and my blood pressure cuff and my orthopedic shoes. And I’m couch surfing. Lord, what’s my life come to? Why can’t I just die?”

“Oh, Francie, I know. I know this is terrible for you. We just need to keep you going a few more weeks. I’m sure a bed’ll open up in a home soon.”

“In a home. I swore I’d never go to a home. Now it’s either that or step in front of a semi.”

“Quit talking like that. There’s no semis going by my building. The only thing you’ll get hit by here is a pot someone throws from a window. Oh, c’mon. We’re both wide awake now. I’ll make some tea.”

***

First Visit

“I’m almost afraid to go in, Edna. Francie’s been here at Assisted Living two weeks now, and we haven’t visited once. Will she be mad, do you think?”

“Probably. But I was so exhausted trying to keep her going until this bed opened up, I needed the break. I think you did too.”

“I know. Not just to catch up on sleep, but to decompress from her ranting and raving about her terrible life.”

“And it has been terrible. But it wasn’t our fault. Are we going to be like that in fifteen years, Irene?”

“Humph. Probably. I’m already apologizing to my kids in advance. Heaven help them if I’m as miserable as Francie.”

"How do we get buzzed in here? All these doors are locked. Do they think people are going to come in and steal the geriatrics?"

"Ha-ha! I doubt it. Maybe they think the geriatrics are going to escape!"

"Oh, look. Here comes a resident. Maybe he can't read that sign there saying don't buzz in people you don't know."

"Maybe he'll think we're residents too."

"Smile. Smile at him. Wave. There we go. Easy as pie! Now, what number is Francie in?"

***

Gravy and Icing

"It was pretty crappy at first. It really was. I got lost all the time. Couldn't figure out the schedule, so I missed meals. But if you don't show up, someone calls your room to make sure you're not sick. So then I'd go down late and at least get something to eat."

"Are the meals okay?"

"Gravy."

"Gravy?"

"Gravy. I don't know who's running this place, but they put gravy on everything. Everything but the desserts, and they're so thick with icing you can barely eat them."

"So the food is lousy. Is everything else lousy too?"

"No, Irene, Edna. Everything isn't lousy, too. Yeah, I complain. I just do that. You know I do. But, it's okay here. I have my own little apartment. I've got my stuff—some of it at least. I know my money's still in the bank. And when I'm lonely, there's always someone I can find to pick a fight with. It's actually pretty good here."

"Pretty good, eh? What more could you ask when you're ninety years old and on your own?"

"I have to admit you were right about a home. It ain't so bad.

A safe place to sleep. Regular food. And you guys. Did I ever say thank you?"

"Aww, Francie, you don't have to thank us."

"I wasn't going to. Just trying to remember if I had. Aww, quit lookin' at me like that. Fine. Thank you. What more could I ask?"

Hope in Three Acts

Katherine Kavanagh Hoffman

ACT I

Sometimes I seek the light but find deep
darkness

darkness blown in like a mist, sitting upon my shoulders
pushing down until my feet
sink
into
the earth

and movement becomes a burden.

I want only to sleep,
to make my escape
as silently
as possible.

Sometimes I repel the darkness and find sweet
light

light, playful as a zephyr, following me wherever I go

Lynn J. Simpson

"I want only to fly across the landscape
as silently as possible."

and lifting me up until my feet
float
above
the earth

and movement becomes a breeze.

I want only to fly
across the landscape
as silently
as possible.

I would like to be constantly in that light,
soaring above the darkness
but life is not like that.

So when I feel my feet
drawn down
into
viscous earth
I lift up my face to the wind and dream of the light
I know
will come
again.

ACT II

Soft sand beneath my feet.
Hot sun, cool breeze, play around my head.
Saltwater pools around me.

I could stay here forever,
imagining that this is all there is,
basking in this new old world.

I do not want to hear about responsibilities—
all that I owe to society,
and all that it offers

I owe nothing
I want nothing

Sometimes survival is enough.

here I survive.

Understatement.

here I thrive as I breathe in the salt air
I absorb the warmth of sand and sun
I am carried away on an ocean breeze.

this is life as it should be-
why should I not strive for it?

far away from the lectures of society
all it owes
and all that I can offer

here for just a moment
I can believe that there is a chance
not just for me but for us all.

ACT III

I will not bend to the wind
for the wind is
not my master.

It cries out
determined
around corners and through cracks.
It chases and teases
but I will not submit.

It may blow against my house against my soul
but it will not overcome.

I will not bend to the wind
for the wind holds
not my destiny.

It calls to me,
enticing,

persuading,
then rattling windows and doors,
seeking a way in.
but I will not succumb.

Let me be!
My spirit has been buffeted by winds
And it has held strong,
for it is wrought from pain and life's uncertainty
it holds firm,
molded by the gentle breezes of Truth which you cannot grasp.

I will hold on to that Truth
and let it carry me on tidal breezes,
I will not let go.

You may seek to entice me,
enslave me,
destroy me

But greater is He that is in me than you who are in this world.
you cannot
you will not
prevail.

So, blow against my house against my soul
you will not overcome.

The Two Notes

Jack Popjes

Jack and his wife Jo spent twenty-four years in Brazil, lived in the Canela's jungle village, learned their unwritten language, developed an alphabet and a learn-to-read program, and left them with a 750-page partial Bible in their language.

The note, signed by the young Canela chief of a new village, was addressed to Jo and me. Soon friends ran up to tell us the same kind of message had been sent to the chief and the leaders of the old, main Canela village where we lived as Bible translating missionaries in Brazil.

We hate you, we reject you, and we never want to see your faces in our village again!

That note hurt! Jo and I had been adopted many years before by Canela families, and the chief of the new village was a younger brother in my extended family. He and I had always gotten along well, and now this.

The previous year when some families talked of starting another village in a location near a different creek, everyone thought it was a good idea since the main village was getting a bit crowded. People from both villages helped to build homes, clear jungle, and plant manioc fields in the new location. But after a year, relationships deteriorated into a political power struggle between the two chiefs, each wanting the most people in his village. And now, after weeks of vicious gossip, the new village chief and leaders had sent notes breaking off all relations with those of us in the old village. According to their oral history, this mutual hate between related villages was a long-standing tradition.

Jo and I talked and prayed together and then sent back the following note:

Dear younger brother chief,

We received your note and read it, and it seems that you hate us and reject us and never want to see us again. We don't know why you feel that way. Maybe someone lied to you about us. We want to remind you that we are of Jesus' group and, therefore, we don't hate you back, nor do we reject you. Instead, we love you now and always will. To prove that we love you, we are sending twenty litres of lamp oil and thirty kilos of salt for you to distribute to all the people in the new village.

Your older brother.

After we sent the note and the gifts we faced a barrage of angry words from our relatives and friends in our village.

"Why did you send them gifts? Don't they hate us all? That's fine. We hate them back. We don't need them. Just let them sit out there in the dark without lamp oil. Let them eat tasteless food. They hate and reject us. Fine, we'll hate and reject them!"

That evening the elders' council called me to attend their meeting in the village plaza to listen to the chief and his counsellors. Each one spoke his piece. All had the same theme: "They hate and reject us, so, therefore, we'll hate and reject them. Also, we don't understand why our friend sent them gifts in exchange for their insult."

Then the chief turned to me and said, "They even treated you that way when all you have ever done is good. You taught them to read and write. You gave them medicine. You've never done anything against any of them. I don't know why you sent them that gift. I hate them on your behalf!" He lapsed into silence, and I asked permission to speak.

"I want to talk to you," I said. "I'm not just going to give you my thoughts about this; I'm going to tell you what Our Great Father in the Sky thinks about this."

I then went on to tell the chief, the elders council, and the village men gathered to listen what Jesus taught about how to treat our enemies. I quoted Jesus and his orders to do good to those who hate us, to feed our enemies, and to let them insult us. They listened, scowling and muttering to each other. In the end, they said they still didn't understand, but they wouldn't be upset with me anymore for having sent the gift.

"Anyway," they said, "it might make that group over there feel ashamed of themselves."

Jo and I went to bed that night with happy hearts—possibly the only happy hearts in either village.

Three days later another note arrived from my younger brother chief—one with a startlingly different message.

We've changed our mind. We don't hate you, and we want to make peace. You can come to our village any time you want.

Whew! Thank you, Jesus!

It still took some months—a centuries-old culture based on mutual hatred doesn't change overnight—but the bad feeling between the villages had begun to dissipate. Eventually, the Canela turned the new village area into a joint manioc raising project, and the inhabitants began returning to the main village.

Jo and I were delighted that besides leading us to translate His Word in the Canela's language, He gave us a perfect public opportunity to translate His Word into action for everyone to see.

After this demonstration, no one in either village had any doubt that change was possible and that a new ethos of mutual love and acceptance could someday replace the old spirit of re-ciprocal hatred and rejection.

The Party

Connie Mae Inglis

"Why do you do this to yourself?" I mutter, staring at my gangly body in the full-length mirror, my knobby knees peeking out of the slate-grey shift dress I splurged on just for this party. The enthusiastic salesperson at the dress shop said I looked stunning, but now, looking in the mirror, the simple dress seems to just accent my awkwardness. Sighing, I recall the conversation with my girlfriend from work a week prior.

"It's Christmas. It'll be fun," she said.

"I'm not much of a party goer," I replied, when what I really should have said was, "I loathe—no, I am allergic to parties."

Why do I kowtow to her effervescence?

My cell phone alarm goes off, reminding me that the taxi will be waiting for me downstairs. Slipping on my slightly worn red pumps, I give myself a "once over" in the mirror.

Hmm. Maybe not so bad. What did Grandma used to say? "Your attitude—your choice."

Rushing out the door with a plate of homemade goodies, I decide to at least try embracing her perspective, wondering if it works for introverts attending extrovert-driven parties.

I arrive late, the party already in high gear, most of the faces unfamiliar, so I find a couch in the corner and silently sip a glass of merlot. From that vantage point I engage in my typical P.O.— participant observation that is—feeling like I'm back in college, taking notes for an anthropology course. In my mind I title my paper, "Party Animalia: How Parties Bring Out the Animal

Instincts—Naturally." I smile at my own cleverness as I focus on my task, content to watch as the music decibels and laughter increase. I spot my friend Stasia and watch her mingle, dancing around the guests in a stunning sequined dress, conversing as she goes. She throws me a smile from across the room but is too engaged to offer more, returning to her free-motion state. I grin and sit back to enjoy the show.

The mental notes on my girlfriend now done, I begin to case out my next subject. Then, through all the flailing legs, I spot her—a child sitting opposite me, her small body lost in the overstuffed armchair, her white-tight legs poking straight off the cushion. She's alone too, although she seems content as well as she brushes the bright pink mane and tail of her "My Little Pony" stuffy, her turned up lips mouthing stifled words. She glances up and our eyes meet. I offer a little wave and smile because her pony is almost as big as she is—and because she looks like a doll, an old-fashioned porcelain one with dark curls, all fancied up in a frilly candy-red dress that fills in the white space around her. She smiles back and suddenly we are the only two people in the room. "I like your stuffy," I mouth and imitate her brushing action. Even from across the room her eyes sparkle as she hugs her stuffy. "Come sit here," I mouth again and pat the couch cushion beside me. She hesitates, looks around, and for a moment I think I've lost her.

But then she slowly slides down from her chair, carefully maneuvers herself and her pink pony around the twisting bodies, and sits down gently on the edge of the couch beside me.

"Hi," I say. "My name is Penny. What's yours?"

"Hope," she smiles softly, balancing her stuffy on her knees.

"What a pretty name."

She looks up, her eyes shining. "Hope Aurora."

"Hope Aurora. I like that. Sort of like how we look at the northern sky, hoping to see the shimmery fluorescent colors and twinkling wonder of the northern lights." She giggles. I like it.

"My mommy says I am a miracle. She calls me her light of hope."

"Wow. Your mommy sounds like a wonderful mommy. Which one is she?"

"That one—in the gold dress. Isn't she pretty?" She waves emphatically to the young brunette who is now slow-dancing with a debonair-looking man, his back to us.

I suck in a breath. My mouth remains open in shock. "That's your mommy?"

"Yes." Her mommy catches Hope's wave and responds with a silent kiss, her green eyes coming to life. She gives me a nod and a grin.

I'm stunned. Her mommy is my friend from work, the hostess of this party. I never pictured her as a mom. I assumed she was single and a partier simply because of her bubbly personality. In fact, I'd never asked her any personal questions. In that brief moment, I realize that I know nothing about Stasia outside of our work world. What a poor friend I've been.

"Isn't she pretty? I helped her pick out that dress."

I give my head a little shake, realizing I'd been staring off into space.

"Yes, you have a beautiful mommy," I say. "You look just like her."

"That's what everyone says."

"It's so true." I turn back to the little girl. She gives me a "what now?" expression, unaware of my social inhibitions.

"Oh hey—did you get something to eat?" I quip. "I have an extra chocolate on my plate. It's a buckeye—filled with creamy peanut butter. Funny name, but they're so yummy." I offer my plate to her and she receives my gift.

"Mmm. This is yummy," she says through a chocolatey grin.

"Don't tell," I whisper. "I'm the one who made them—and now I'm the one eating them. They're too good to resist." She licks the chocolate off her thumb and finger and sits back in the seat.

"Nice shoes," I say, now noticing her red, sequined flats jutting out. "They're like Dorothy's from the Wizard of Oz. Have you ever clicked them together?" I joke. She tips her head, giving me a blank stare. "No, I suppose not. You're a little young for cackling witches and scary flying monkeys."

She says nothing, still looking perplexed.

"It's the story of a young girl like you—well, maybe a little older. And she gets lost and can't find her way home. But her shoes, like your shoes, help her get home. Her shoes—and her friends."

Hope sits forward, her eyes bright. "Do the red shoes help her find friends?"

"Umm. Maybe. I never really thought about it. But she makes some nice friends."

Looking down at her doll, Hope says, "I miss my friends."

"Sorry?"

"My mommy and I just moved into this part of the city."

"Well . . ." I look down, unsure of what to say next. "Look," I say, pointing to my own shoes then turning to Hope. "I have red shoes too."

She peeks over the edge of the couch and lets out a little squeal. "Ooo, yours are pretty too."

"Maybe . . ." I say, offering her my biggest smile. "Maybe we could be friends. We could be the red shoes sisters."

The gleam returns to Hope's emerald eyes. Now I lean back, and she mirrors my actions.

"Well, little Red Shoes Sister," I say, "what should we talk about now?"

"I like red," she begins, "but my favorite color is pink. Mommy couldn't find any pink shoes."

"Ah. That's why you have Pinkie Pie. Is she your favourite?"

"Yup," Hope says, giving her pony a tight squeeze and then looking at my empty plate. "Do you have any more of those eyeballs? I think Pinkie Pie would like one."

"Eyeballs?"

"Yeah, those chocolate things you brought."

"Oh, you mean buckeyes." I smile and give the food table a quick once-over. "Looks like they're all gone. Sorry." I turn back to see Hope's smile become a frown, and immediately an idea pops into my head—and an opportunity to develop a friendship. "Tell you what. Maybe one day I could come over and we could make some together."

The little girl squeals, and I laugh because she's clapping not only her hands but also her shoes. "Oh, can we? I'd like that. Pinkie Pie would like that too."

"Well, I'd have to ask your mommy."

"Oh, she'll say yes. I know she will." Hope's joy reminds me of her mother, and I can't help but smile.

"Okay, well first thing Monday morning I'll ask her. Maybe she could join us."

"Yes. Yes. Yes."

"That is, if she has red shoes too."

"Oh, yes. I'm sure she does. And I could show you all the pink things I have." At that, Hope chatters away about her room; I soak in her love for life, and she responds to my curiosity.

All the while I consider what I would've missed—what I would be missing—if I hadn't followed my grandmother's advice and said yes to Stasia's party invitation. Finding Hope reminded me that you can never predict what the future holds when you choose the right attitude.

The Hope Tree

Katherine Kavanagh Hoffman

Once upon a time there was a village. And in the middle of the village, there was a garden. And in the garden, there was a tree. No one knew when the tree had been planted. It had been there as long as anyone could remember, and its branches spread over the village like a protective canopy. They provided shade in the hot sun and shelter during storms. And the leaves spread out just far enough that the village received the perfect amount of rain and snow to provide moisture but never flooding, sunshine that warmed but never burned, breezes that cooled but never became harsh winds. The village always seemed "just right." No harshness, but a temperate and comfortable climate which seemed to make the inhabitants quite temperate and comfortable, too.

After many years, an emperor, who had extended his kingdom far and wide, conquered the country in which this village was found. His goal was power and control, and he desired to extend that power and control as far and wide as he could. He was a tyrant and liked nothing more than to know he was bringing misery and suffering into the lives of his conquered peoples.

A report came back to him that the people of this small village continued to thrive in spite of the harsh measures that the emperor had imposed on this newly conquered country. As usual, he had sent his soldiers into every village. They imposed strict order, collected high dues, and limited the freedom and movement of the people. This alone was generally enough to subdue the already war-tired people; however, this did not seem to be the case in this one small village. The emperor was angry. This had never happened before. He was also intrigued. What was keeping his power from ruining the lives of the people in this insignificant village? He called for his generals and questioned them, but they could not explain it. He sent his most trusted ministers and advisors to the town, but they, too, came back without answers. It was infuriating. This village seemed to be immune to his influence—and hardly concerned that it was meddling with a very powerful and angry sovereign.

These were seriously less than comfortable circumstances for the emperor. His word was law, his law was kept through fear, and he thrived on the feeling of power that gave him. No one crossed him. Besides, a happy village could undermine all his efforts to enforce his will on his conquered lands. What if word got out? That possibility could not be tolerated. He sent orders to his militia that they ensure the villagers be stripped of any and all privileges that may have been overlooked, that all businesses be closed—except those of importance to his sol-diers—and that no entertainment of any sort be permitted. He would have removed all food and water from the villagers, too, if he had dared. But he needed workers, and he knew he could not starve them if he wanted his work to be done. But even with all the additional hardships, the villagers appeared to be unmoved.

This was a dilemma! The emperor was really angry now. He determined that he would have to go to the village himself and find out what was going on. This made him even more angry, as he sorely disliked being inconvenienced. And this was a major inconvenience. How incompetent were his generals? His sol-diers? They should have been able to deal with this themselves and not call him away from important domestic business.

He determined to go in disguise so he could look for answers without drawing undue attention to himself. He rode his own horse and travelled with only a small contingency decked out to

Lynn J. Simpson

"Throughout the entire kingdom, these trees began to grow far faster than any normal tree ever would. Within days, they had spread their branches, creating canopy after canopy across the kingdom."

look like road-weary travellers. He was not taking any chances of being recognized.

As he travelled through the countryside, he was heartened to see that his usual strategies had subdued this newly conquered country: the people were downtrodden, many homes and fields were destroyed. Other villages seemed to be suffering as they should. It encouraged him. Surely this one little village could not hold out for too much longer.

He was chagrined, however, to find that he recognized the village before he even entered it. While the surrounding land had been laid to waste, green grasses and shrubbery were in view as soon as he reached its edge. Birds were singing, and he could even spot a squirrel or two. His mood became darker as the scene brightened. As he entered the town, he saw that although the villagers were thin and dressed in ragged clothing, they still found the energy to greet the newly arrived stranger with courtesy and smiles, offering what they had—food, shelter, and a place to sleep—even though they had little for themselves. The emperor smiled back, but behind his smile he was seething. How dare they? How could they? How was this possible? Why was this tiny insignificant village not destroyed?

He moved through the village and, refusing all offers, returned to his own encampment on a hill nearby. That night he slept fitfully, filled with loathing for the little town and its inhabitants, determined to bring them fully under his control and to find out what was preventing him from doing so.

The next morning he walked through the village to see what he could discover. Even with the businesses closed, the inhabitants still seemed busy. They consulted with one another, shared what they had, and spoke of plans for the future when the businesses and shops would be reopened and they would once more prosper. In the meantime, they organized themselves as best they could to meet the needs of each and every one. He noted that they did not seem worried, though they were realistic about what was happening. More than once, he overheard them wishing him well, toasting him, and sending up prayers that he might relent from his campaign of destruction.

Their behaviour was so strange. What was wrong with these people? Couldn't they see the troublesome position they were in? Why were they behaving so differently than the other people in their country? He could not put his finger on it.

He remained encamped near the village for some time. Day after day, he wandered through the streets, trying to understand what was happening, but he came no closer to the truth.

Then, one day, he sat to rest in the ancient garden. He had not paid much attention to it up to this point, being not overly fond of flowers and greenery. But as he rested there, he began to feel something changing within himself. He did not like the feeling. His worry and anger began to ebb away and seemed suddenly quite pointless. He started to relax and could feel the beginnings of a smile on his lips. He shook his head and frowned, working hard to escape this unwelcome sensation. And then he looked up. He saw that he was sitting under the shelter of an enormous tree with branches that stretched out far above him, creating a canopy that reached out to the edge of the village. He could still see the sun peeking through the leaves but, though it was midsummer and there were no clouds in the sky, he was not scorched by it. Rather, he felt a comfortable warmth and a light breeze. It was enjoyable. He started to smile again, then got up quickly and shook himself all over. Enjoyable? Warmth and summer breezes were not enjoyable. Power was enjoyable! Strength was enjoyable! Control was enjoyable! He repeated these ideas over and over again in his mind. He did not understand how or why but, somehow, this tree at the centre of the village was at the centre of his problem.

Now that he had become suspicious about the tree, he did not want to spend any more time in the village than absolutely necessary. But he still needed to know more about the tree to discover if it really could be the source of his problems. He would get as much information as he could for the rest of the day and then leave quickly before this tree could have any greater effect on him. He walked through the village, avoiding the garden as much as he could, for he felt that the worst effects were found closest to the base of the tree. He asked everyone he met what they knew about the tree: How long had it been there? Who had planted it? What kind of tree was it? No one seemed able to tell him very much. By the end of the day, he had no more information than he had begun with, but all his instincts told him that, somehow, this tree was the reason for the resilience of the village. And the emperor had learned to trust his instincts.

He left the next morning, determined that the tree must be destroyed. Consulting with his generals, he sent their troops out to the village to do the deed, but no matter what they tried, nothing could destroy the tree. Axes did not make a mark, nor saws, nor anything that would cut. Some smaller branches were pulled off, but they grew back within hours. Whatever was done to the tree, it remained unharmed.

The emperor was furious. "That tree must go! When it is gone, I will have the village, and that will give me the whole kingdom forever. I will stop at nothing to get rid of that tree!"

He called his generals together and told them, "The tree must be burned to the ground. That is the only way to get rid of it once and for all."

His generals looked at one another in trepidation. "But, sire, it is in the middle of the town! And the branches spread out over the whole area. How can we contain the flames? The fire will destroy everything nearby. There will be no village left when this deed is done."

The emperor rubbed his hands together. He grinned fiendishly. "Then our problem will be solved. Go! Do as I have commanded."

The following morning, the villagers saw a new group of soldiers entering the garden, but these ones brought stacks of wood and vats of oil rather than saws and axes. All around the tree, they placed as much wood as possible to create as hot a fire as they could, as if fearful that the wood of the tree would not burn otherwise. They doused the wood with oil to ensure that a good burn would follow. They were not taking any chances. They had been warned that failure would come at the cost of their own lives. It was a sombre group who set about their work.

The emperor found a vantage point above his encampment, anxious to witness his victory fulfilled.

When all was ready, a torchbearer arrived. He gingerly touched the burning torch to the wood around the tree. The oil ignited quickly. Soon the fuel was spent, and the fire was licking the huge trunk of the tree. Singe marks began to appear, and the leaves crumpled and began to fall, succumbing to the extreme heat. On the hillside, the emperor could see the smoke and the flames slowly climbing up the trunk of the tree.

"It's working! I knew that fire was the answer. Soon the tree will be destroyed, and all will be as I have envisioned it!"

Back in the village, the inhabitants were beginning to gather around the garden. Instead of drawing back, as the soldiers were doing, the villagers were staying as close as they could to the tree, staying only as far back as the intensity of the heat forced them to do. They had been warned to leave, as there was a strong likelihood that their village would be destroyed along with the tree itself. But the villagers seemed unconcerned. They kept their vigil, as close to the tree as they could manage, following the progression of the flames with their eyes while shielding them from the heat of the flames.

Just as the fire reached so high that it began to lick the canopy of leaves and branches itself, something strange began to happen. As the fire touched the highest limbs of the tree, they began to spread apart, almost folding back from the trunk, leaning towards the ground below. As they did, an opening appeared in the centre of the tree. The soldiers, fearful that the limbs would fall to the ground and crush and burn them, ran off, leaving their posts entirely. They were followed by a strange popping sound that convinced them the fire was overtaking them and destroying everything in its path. From his vantage point on the hillside, the emperor could clearly see all that was happening. Something was coming out of the hole in the centre of the tree. No, not one, but many things were emerging, popping up into the sky like popcorn jumping out of hot oil in a skillet, popping in every direction. Hundreds, perhaps thousands, of seed pods! Out of the tree and into the air they rose. Caught by the wind, they travelled far and wide. Everywhere they landed, new trees sprouted. Throughout the entire kingdom, these trees began to grow far faster than any normal tree ever would. Within days, they had spread their branches, creating canopy after canopy across the kingdom. Every village, every town, every farm now had its own tree. And, like the original tree, its progeny brought shelter and peace to everyone under its limbs.

In the little village itself, a new tree rose from the cinders of the old, and though the old one had burned right down to the ground, no harm was done to the village or its inhabitants at all. "Old magic," they said to one another with a knowing nod.

As for the emperor, when he realised what was happening, he turned his back on that troublesome kingdom, fighting off the feeling of peace and well-being which continued to badger him, until he reached the borders of his own dark kingdom, where he could brood in anger and misery as much as he chose to do so. He never attempted to expand his kingdom again. And, although he never could understand the power of the tree, he determined that it would be safer to stay far away from it. Yet, from time to time, he would waken from dreams, rub his eyes, shake his head, and try to shrug off the desire to go back to the village, find the tree once again, and sit beneath its leafy canopy.

And the people of the village and its surrounding kingdom lived hopefully ever after.

Healing Skies

Joy Bailey

Ascend, celestial sphere, above distress,
Fair blue, or stormy sea of endless mirth,
From my harassed perspective on this earth,
Give peace of mind, and all my cares suppress.

If nature can appease unquiet minds
Then sapphire skies will hopelessness console.
Sweet indigo expanse sustains my soul,
Vitality and life return in kind.

When angry clouds and wind reflect my mood,
My cry is swallowed up by thunder's roar.
To all my rants God shows His magnitude,
It's then I grant He's my superior.

Yet I do not resent this raging feud.
I know myself amidst our tug of war.

Lynn J. Simpson

"If nature can appease unquiet minds
Then sapphire skies will hopelessness console."

Hope Came in a Box

Tina Markeli

Doreen slumped in her chair. Christmas was coming. The past year had been a perfect storm. She and her husband, Charles, were in a new place on a small island in Southeast Asia with none of their familiar things, none of their trusted coworkers nearby, none of their familiar Christmas decorations waiting to be hung on a tree. Worse, they were facing their first Christmas as "empty nesters" with both their daughters on the other side of the world. Her nest and heart, usually warm and full of Christmas joy, felt as empty and useless as the discarded banana leaf wrapper from last night's supper drying out in the wastebasket beside her.

Should we even bother trying to decorate the house for Christmas? I know that Christmas is about Jesus and His birth, not things or decorations," she chided herself. *"Still, shouldn't I put up some decorations and make a statement that Christmas is a truly great event? The majority of the people around us don't know the story of God's gift of a Saviour. Maybe a few decorations would help us share the good news.* On this early-December afternoon, Doreen was finding a wide gulf between the secure knowledge of God's great love stored in her head and the discouragement threatening to overwhelm her heart.

Doreen fled to their upstairs bedroom, the only air-conditioned room in the house, and opened her journal. She settled in her favourite chair, letting the light of the single window fall on the pages in her lap. Maybe a review of the year, how she and

Charles had come to this day, this place, would help her to face this Christmas so unlike any Christmas she had ever known.

The year had begun with turmoil at the Bible school on another island. Charles was a lecturer and Doreen the school treasurer. Conflict with the school's director had led to hurt feelings and strained relationships. More turmoil would engulf and rock them before the situation was finally resolved. Nevertheless, God had brought reconciliation. A ray of sunshine poked a tentative finger in her direction.

Endless government paperwork for visas, work permits, police permits, and driver licences in a country not sympathetic to Christians had added to their stress. Thankfully, Charles took care of dealing with the officials who sent him from one desk to another in the maze of government bureaucracy. While Doreen did not accompany him on these missions, she shared the emotional strain.

An early-March journal entry told how, on a Friday evening, Doreen's brother's voice came over the phone, his tone serious. "Mom fell. She is very weak. Perhaps you should come." For the first time in twenty years, her brother was asking for help caring for their parents. The weight of his concern settled on her spirit like an overloaded market basket.

Doreen launched into overdrive. Within forty-eight hours she had made arrangements to cover her responsibilities at the Bible school, planned meals for Charles and Sally, their daughter who was finishing grade twelve, and packed her bags. She was amazed to find airline tickets to Vancouver, at half price, for Monday evening—surely a gift from God. Getting her exit/re-entry permit in only one session at the immigration office was nothing short of a miracle. She recalled boarding the plane after midnight to find her assigned seat was in business class, with a generously wide seat and a footrest for her legs, all on a half-price economy ticket—another God gift. Before the seatbelt sign was turned off, she was fast asleep.

Three weeks of daily visits in her Mom's hospital room

were a once-in-a-lifetime treasure. But Doreen had to return to Charles and Sally. Forcing a smile, she said, "Goodbye, Mom. I'll see you in the morning." They both knew it would be no earthly morning. She managed to reach the privacy of her brother's pickup truck before her tears spilled uncontrollably. Fresh tears fell on the journal page.

Journal entries for April and May told of the financial crisis at the Bible school that consumed all of her time and emotional resources. As treasurer, she could not postpone her duties. At the same time, Sally was graduating from high school. Sally's older sister had come from Canada. Doreen wanted to spend time with her daughters, to celebrate this major milestone, but felt compelled to put in long hours to take care of the crisis at the Bible school. Charles and the girls didn't complain. They just got things done at home. Their support was wonderful even as everyone felt torn. Watching the girls walk into the airport, headed for Canada and college, Doreen's heart alternated between pride in her daughters and despair over their absence. Now the full width of the Pacific Ocean plus the Rocky Mountains separated her from her girls. But there was no time to dwell on the loss.

The phone rang. "Doreen, Mom is in heaven," her brother said, his voice wavering. "My wife was with her when she passed, so she wasn't alone, just as she hoped." Doreen thanked him for caring for their Mom. Words of comfort came out of her mouth while her feelings went numb. Work responsibilities and finances would not allow her to go back to Canada for the funeral. She set the journal aside to deal with the fresh tears.

She resumed her reading. She and Charles had long planned to transfer to another island to assist young Bible school graduates working in new locations. The movers descended on their house, packed their boxes and furniture into crates, and loaded everything onto a large transport truck. A large tarp was secured over the load to protect the crates from dirt and rain. Their possessions departed for the harbour. Charles and Doreen would take the ferry a few days later. Ready or not, they were being catapulted into a new chapter of life.

The journal told how, on their arrival on the island, they had gone directly to the small house that Charles had arranged for them and waited for their shipment to arrive. They slept on the floor and declared war on the cockroaches that had claimed the empty house for themselves. They made tea, slurped instant noodles, and ate overly spicy meals from local food stalls. "Our things will come on Tuesday," was their weapon of hope.

Tuesday evening came, but no shipment. The cell phone they had brought did not connect to the local networks. They were used to waiting. "Tomorrow," they said and smiled at each other.

Wednesday morning, a young co-worker arrived on his motorcycle with a cryptic message. "Call the office of the Bible school you just left." Charles jumped on the back of the motorcycle for a ride to the nearest telephone kiosk a few kilometres away.

The words of her journal seemed to darken as she remembered Charles's grim face when he walked in the door. Their shipment would never arrive. Somewhere between the docks of the capital city and the port on their little island, the ship had disappeared, taking their belongings with it. The shipping agent would only say that the boat had gone down, but he gave no details. Doreen pictured fish at the bottom of the strait feasting, at that very moment, on her precious Christmas decorations. Friends said the ship had probably been hijacked, in which case her Christmas decorations were likely being hawked in some market stall. It made no difference. They had no Christmas decorations, no family to join the celebration, no western friends to share their traditions, no recordings of Christmas music— nothing to evoke the familiar, comforting Christmas feelings.

She returned to her journal. Thankfully they had taken insurance for the replacement costs of the shipment. Of course, some things could never be replaced: the pictures Charles had drawn before they were married and the antique rocking chair with its comforting squeak which Charles had given her when Sally was born. Her favourite blue-and-white shawl was gone too.

"It's only stuff," they told each other bravely. "Things can be replaced. We know God wants to turn this into something good." However, feelings do not always immediately match our brave, faith-filled words. Feelings often need time to accept reality.

She could still feel the adrenaline rush of the major shopping trips. The appliance salesman could hardly conceal his eagerness to serve this western couple who purchased a stove, refrigerator, and washing machine in one order. The furniture store was equally helpful. They purchased dishes, pots, pans, cutlery, kitchen tools, towels, sheets, pillows. Would these things truly replace what they had lost?

Memories of repeated trips to the second-hand market brought a smile as she read on. They had found a round kitchen table with four matching wooden chairs. With the addition of plastic chairs, they could seat ten people around that table to accommodate their local co-workers and so encourage each other. Her treadle sewing machine was another second-hand market find. The frequent interruptions in electricity no longer disrupted her sewing. God had not forgotten them.

She read more journal entries from those first weeks in this housing development, still under construction. Daily shopping excursions brought useful information. "Those vegetables are cute," the shopkeeper said one morning. "Cute?" Doreen repeated. "I would say beautiful." "Cute is the word we use here," he assured her. She made a mental note about changes in her vocabulary.

The main street of the complex boasted just one store that sold western items like bread, margarine, and small jars of peanut butter. Other storefronts sat empty, waiting for future residents and entrepreneurs. Doreen thought her soul was like those storefronts—empty—waiting for she didn't know what. She missed their coworkers back on the other island. She missed her Mom. She missed her daughters. She missed the familiar routines of the Bible school. She missed friends who spoke English.

She closed her journal. What a year! No wonder she didn't feel like Christmas. On December twenty-first they would fly to visit friends at the Bible school on the other island.

"Is it worth decorating the house if we won't be here on Christmas Day?" she asked Charles. "We don't have any decorations. I don't even know where to look for some. I haven't seen any in the stores downtown."

"Let's try and do *something*," Charles countered. Always practical, he found a small, bare tree branch and anchored it in a vase. "You can make some of those three-dimensional origami stars," he encouraged.

As she cut plain white paper into strips and folded them, Doreen comforted herself with memories. *Bless Willie, Charles' friend who taught me to make these. Then there was that night when Mom and I worked until 1 a.m. trying again and again until we got the instructions right so we could teach a group of ladies the next day. I'm glad Sally and her sister learned to make them. I wonder how many of these stars I have made over the years? I've used them on Christmas trees, as bows on gifts, hung them on mobiles. People sure like them.* The memories helped. She willed a smile. *It's Christmas. God's gift to us is worth celebrating.*

A knock at the door interrupted her thoughts. The mailman was holding a small box, the wrapping paper secured with lots of scotch tape. The return address was that of the old Bible school. Her fingers tore at the paper with an unfamiliar eagerness. Inside was a framed, cross-stitched Christmas hanging that her best friend, Leila, had made. "Noel," it announced in the familiar red and green. A note said, "I'm sorry this didn't make the package we sent as a group. Merry Christmas!" Doreen's spirit gave a hopeful leap.

Then her mind puzzled. What did Leila mean about a package?

"A package, what package?" Doreen asked Leila via email, after expressing her sincere thanks.

"We know you lost all your Christmas decorations," came the reply. "We wanted you to have something familiar for Christmas. Each one of us here at the Bible school took one of our decorations, something you have seen in our homes, and sent them to you. Haven't you received that package?"

The larger package would not arrive for another month. Yet, knowing that their coworkers cared and had sacrificed their decorations helped Doreen and Charles to look ahead. Hope had arrived in one small, carefully wrapped box.

Hansje Leaves Holland to Go to Canada

Jack Popjes

When it was nearly time to leave Holland and go to Canada, Papa hired some carpenters to come and measure the furniture and make some big shipping crates. He wanted to take the extra-long bed, the linen closet with the big mirror, the good chairs and table, some living room furniture, and especially the baby crib, the playpen, and the baby changing table that he had made himself. And, of course, the wall clock they had bought as a wedding present for themselves.

It was exciting to be getting ready, but it wasn't going to be easy to leave. Hansje found that out one day when Papa came in to eat some lunch. He had just started eating when the phone rang in the hallway. Papa went out, chewing and swallowing quickly so he could answer it. A few minutes later, he was back, his face looking pale and white and his lips pressed tightly together. His eyes were flashing with anger.

"The government tax people just found some more taxes we need to pay," he said to Mama, "but they won't let me sell the house until we have paid most of them." Suddenly he ran from the room, down the hall, and Hansje could hear him vomiting in the bathroom.

The next day Papa went to the bank to borrow some money to pay the taxes. Hansje guessed the bank didn't want to give him very much money because the next thing he knew the carpenters were gone, leaving only a small, flat crate—just enough for the bed, crib, playpen, linen closet and the clock.

The week before they left, Papa sold all the rest of their furniture and paid some of the taxes. Then he finally sold the house and paid the rest of the taxes. But now they didn't have enough money to pay for the boat tickets. Hansje knew that because he heard Papa ask his younger brother Teus if he would loan him some money. Finally, they had enough to buy the tickets.

On Monday Papa packed the last five pieces of furniture into the flat crate, nailed it shut, and sent it off to the ship on a truck. That night the whole family packed up their suitcases, left their empty house, and spent the night at Opa and Oma's house, Papa's parents.

Lynn J. Simpson

"The land where he had hidden in swamps and under the floor of his house during the war to save his life."

Then, at last, on Tuesday morning, July 11, 1950, they all got up early, had breakfast after which they prayed together with Oma and Opa and the rest of the uncles and aunts that came to say goodbye. Then they loaded their stuff and themselves into a rented car and drove away. They left Hilversum, where Hansje, his brother, and sisters were born and had lived all their lives, and drove sixty-five kilometres to Rotterdam. There they would board an emigrant ship called the Volendam.

There was a lot of confusion once they got to the dock at Rotterdam. Papa had to stand in a long line with tickets, papers, x-ray photos and passports, while Mama sat on a big suitcase, holding baby Annie, surrounded by other suitcases that Hansje and his brother and sisters were sitting on. They were not the only people sitting on suitcases. The whole dock, the full length of the ship, was covered with women and kids sitting on suitcases waiting for the men to finish standing in line and for the signal to climb the long gangplank to the deck.

After a long time, baby Annie started to cry because she was hungry. So Mama put a shawl around her shoulders and front and breastfed her for a while until she was quiet again and went to sleep. A mother sitting on a suitcase near them also had a crying baby, and she was also trying to breastfeed her baby, but soon the mother was crying too. "What's the matter?" Mama asked her.

"I don't have enough breast milk," she sobbed, "I can't fix a bottle. The bottle and the stuff for making bottle milk is packed tightly in the suitcase."

"I have lots of milk," Mama said. "Would you like me to feed your baby?"

"Oh, would you? the other mother said. "Please feed her." So Mama gave Annie to the mother to hold while she took her baby and fed it. Soon it was asleep, too. The other mother asked Mama how old Annie was.

"Annie is five months old," Mama said. "Bea is two, Wobbie is six, Jannie is eight and Hansje is twelve years old."

And Mama and Papa are really old, Hansje thought, *thirty-six and forty.*

After many hours, they let down the gangway, and everyone trooped onto the ship carrying their suitcases. Mama and the little kids were in a big cabin in the middle of the ship with some other mothers and little kids. Papa and Hansje and all the other men and boys were in a large dormitory in the front end of the ship. It took a long time to get everyone settled, but then the ship began to move, and Hansje and Papa went up on the deck to look. It was fun watching all the people waving from the dock, and he loved seeing the ships on either side of the harbor with cranes loading the ships and people working on the dock.

When they left the river channel and entered the open sea, Papa and Hansje walked to the very back of the boat, the stern, and leaned on the railing watching the land slowly get farther and farther away.

Hansje looked at Papa. He was holding onto the railing with both hands, staring beyond the white foamy wake behind the ship to the low, black shoreline as it faded into the twilight of evening.

Suddenly the bell rang calling everyone to go to the dining room for supper. But Papa didn't move. Hansje looked up at Papa's face; his eyes were glaring at the land where he was born and where he had lived for forty years.

The land where he grew up in Opa and Oma's house with six brothers and two sisters. The land where he had married Mama and had six kids, one of which died while still a baby. The land where he had hidden in swamps and under the floor of his house during the war to save his life. The land where he had quit school at twelve years old and gone to work and had worked ever since, for twenty-eight years.

And now he was leaving it all. He owned nothing but the clothes on his back and a few bits of furniture. His own country had taken everything from him except his family.

As the last black strip of land disappeared over the horizon,

Papa cleared his throat and spat a great gob of disgust at his country. Then he took a deep breath of clean, fresh, salty air and said to Hansje "And now we are going to Canada!"

He took Hansje by the hand and walked briskly to the dining room. Hansje was excited to be on the way, finally. He couldn't wait to get to Canada.

Mrs. Morton's Garden

Katherine Kavanagh Hoffman

After I retired, I lived in my condo for a few years before deciding that I wanted a change. That was when I moved into a seniors' assisted living building. I didn't need any assistance yet, please understand; I was on the independent living floor. But I did sign up for my evening meal in the dining room. The food was good, and it was nice to have a menu to choose from, but I did everything else myself. And I mean everything. I wasn't over the hill yet.

Of course, there were a lot of top-of-the-hill folks in the building, eating all their meals in the dining room and getting help with almost everything. And a few were definitely on their way down the hill, too, if you know what I mean.

One of the top-of-the-hill folks was a woman called Mrs. Morton. She was an old gal—must have been in her late 80s, I'm sure, but spry and active, with a twinkle in her eye. The first time I met her, she was dressed up to the nines, waiting for the bus in the foyer of the building. (Our building has its own bus. Very swanky place, you know.) I was heading down to the 7-11 for my favourite bag of chips. I nodded politely going by, but she stopped me.

"Hello there. You're Karla, aren't you?" I couldn't help but wonder how she knew my name, but then I guess there isn't much to do when you got as old as she was but find out about your neighbours.

"Yes, that's right. Just moved in last week. And you?"

"I am Mrs. Morton."

She said it kindly. I thought it was a bit old-fashioned, though, to just tell me her last name. But I figured I looked pretty darn young to her. That is a family trait. My hair is still only salt and pepper at 73.

"Well, hello, Mrs. Morton." I thought I'd humour her. "And where are you off to this afternoon?"

"I'm going to tend to my garden," she said with a smile.

Oh, boy, I thought. She looks okay on the outside, but I guess she's a little off on the inside. Not unusual with these old girls, I suppose.

"Would you like to come along?"

I shook my head and smiled. "Oh, no. You go ahead and have a good time. The little garden on my balcony is enough for me." I got out of there pretty quick, chuckling to myself a bit as I went.

Well, anytime I happened to be going that way after lunch, there was Mrs. Morton, all dressed up, waiting for the bus. Monday to Friday, you could set your clock by her. And each time she saw me, we had the same conversation. I'd ask her where she was off to, and she'd tell me she was going to tend her garden, or water it, or sow some seeds in it. Always the same kind of answer, with a little smile and that twinkle in her eye. It would have been funny if it hadn't been so sad. I'd guess she was heading off to the mall for a little outing, maybe to the dollar store or coffee at the food fair. She always asked me to come along. I'd thank her and say no, then carry on with my business.

It was coming on spring, that first year I was living there, and I hadn't seen Mrs. Morton waiting for the bus at her usual post for about a week. When I asked Denise, the receptionist, she told me that Mrs. Morton had taken sick—pneumonia, one of those things that can give an old girl a real run for her money, you know—and she was in the hospital. She was doing alright, but they were keeping her in for a while just to be sure. You don't want to take chances with someone that old. It was another couple of weeks before I saw her again. She was just coming back, being wheeled inside in a chair. She looked pale, but she still had a twinkle in her eye. A little less bright than usual, maybe. I almost asked her about her garden, but thought better of it. I didn't want to be insensitive, after all.

Well, just after she arrived back, a lot of deliveries started coming to the building. Baskets of fruit, muffins and cookies, flowers—you name it. Every couple of days, something would arrive. A lot of the food ended up in the common areas. They were being sent to Mrs. Morton, you see, but she couldn't have eaten half the stuff, there was so much of it. She wasn't even coming down for meals yet, being still kind of weak from her illness, and I doubt she was eating a whole lot of anything. So, she was sharing with the rest of us in the building. The thing that caught my curiosity, though, were the cards attached to all these gifts. They always said "From Mrs. Morton's Garden."

Very odd. I had figured that the garden was in the old lady's head. Now it turned out that the garden could bake, shop, and pick flowers. Who ever heard of a garden picking its own flowers?

I asked Denise about it one day, nonchalant-like, but she just gave me a look and a smile.

"That's Mrs. Morton's story to tell, Karla. After all, it is her garden!" Infuriating. But what could I do? I thought of inviting myself into Mrs. Morton's apartment, but I had never been there before, so I figured it might seem a bit forward. Instead, I waited. I knew she would be back downstairs eventually.

It took a few weeks, but one day, there she was, waiting for the bus just like usual, as if nothing had happened—though this time she was sitting while she waited. Just to reserve her strength, I guess. She looked a whole lot better than the last time I saw her: pretty good for an old lady who had just fought off pneumonia. And that twinkle was still there—a bit subdued yet, but obviously working its way back to its usual shine. We greeted each other, also as usual, but she had a bit more to say this time.

"I haven't been able to tend to my garden for so long. Oh, how I miss it! And I can only go once a week for now. The doctor says I need to take it slow. But I can go more again when I am feeling stronger."

I hesitated, then asked the question that had been tickling my tongue for so long. "So, Mrs. Morton—exactly what is this garden of yours?"

She looked up and smiled. "Why don't you come along and see for yourself?"

I had passed up on this invitation so many times that I almost started shaking my head out of habit, but then I caught myself and changed the shake into a nod.

"Well, okay then—I guess I could come today. Nothing else on the go. Just let me grab my hat and purse. Hold the bus for me."

I scampered off as fast as I could. Don't laugh, I can still scamper pretty good! I grabbed what I needed and was back beside her just as the bus was pulling up.

It was not a long ride, but long enough for Mrs. Morton to tell me her story.

"I was a war bride, you know."

I nodded, but I hadn't known. I'd never thought to ask.

"I came to Canada in 1946, just 18 years old. So young. Maybe too young to be a bride, but war can make you old before your time. All my teenage years were during wartime. Instead of dances and movies, we had curfews and rationing—when we were lucky. I grew up in fear. We saw hunger, injustice, fighting, death. We learned to make ourselves small. We learned to be quiet, to make ourselves out to be insignificant. It was safer that way . . ." Mrs. Morton paused, lost in her memories. She shook herself and looked straight at me.

"And then, Curtis brought me here. To a big city. To a country that did not speak my language. To people who were so different from anyone I had ever known. Everything was strange to me. And, at first, I didn't feel any safer than I had in my village during the war. I still felt small and insignificant. I tried to hide, just as I had done then. When I had my first child, I realized that this was not the kind of life I wanted for my family—or for myself. The war had changed things for the worse for so many people. It had destroyed so many people. But that did not mean we could not change things for the better. Start again. Build a new life, a better life. Those of us who made it through owed it to those who had not. It took me a long time to realize that."

She looked at me long and hard. "But once I did, I was determined to learn, to grow. So, I took classes. I learned to speak English—and some French—and I learned to read and write in English. It was very hard. Even the alphabet was different. But I knew it was the only way to build a new life in this new place. Curtis was a great encouragement. He never wanted me to be something I was not, but he always wanted me to be whatever I wanted to be. When our children were grown and had moved out on their own, I decided I didn't want to sit still! I wanted to keep growing. I wanted to help others grow. I had always loved gardening." There was that twinkle again! "We had flowers in the front and vegetables in the back of our little house. But now I was ready to grow a different kind of garden. Not a garden that grows in the ground, but the kind that will keep growing long into the future, long after I am gone. So, I called the school near our home—the school our children had gone to many years before. And I asked if they needed a gardener."

The bus lurched to a stop, and I looked up. We were in front of a school. An elementary school.

"This is where your garden is?"

I still didn't get it. I knew some schools had community gardens, but this old bird certainly couldn't be digging and planting, even if she did twenty years ago. Especially now—no strength for sure. What kind of garden could she help with?

"Yes," replied Mrs. Morton as she made her way down to the sidewalk with a little help from the driver. "This is my garden."

We walked up the path to the door, opened it, and followed

the signs towards the office. The hallways were quiet. All the kids were in class, I suppose. Before we got to the office (Visitors Please Report Here!), a woman stepped out and came towards us.

"Mrs. Morton! Welcome back. So glad you are feeling better." She gave her a hug and turned to me. "I'm Janet—the principal here. Welcome. Any friend of Mrs. Morton's is a friend of ours!"

I introduced myself and shook her hand. Janet turned back to Mrs. Morton.

"We have a surprise for you today, Mrs. Morton. A little assembly in the gym. The children were so happy to hear you were coming back, we thought a celebration was in order."

Janet took Mrs. Morton's arm and led us down the corridor and away from the office. I could hear a buzz of voices as we approached two large doors, the kind of buzz you hear when people are trying to be quiet but aren't doing a very good job of it.

Someone was standing by the doors. A teacher, I suppose. Janet nodded at her, and she headed inside. I heard her say, "Okay, everyone, remember what we practised. Ms. Edel is coming down the hall with Mrs. Morton." The hum grew louder, with scattered applause. Then, to my surprise, complete quiet. I didn't think kids were capable of that.

Janet—Ms. Edel, that is—led Mrs. Morton through the door. I hung back a bit. I wasn't going to steal the limelight. I was close enough to see and hear what happened next, though. Those kids stood up all together, and in one voice they said, "Welcome back, Mrs. Morton! Your garden has missed you!"

Well, I'm a pretty tough hen, but I had tears in my eyes, I don't mind telling you. And when I saw the sign at the back of the gym, written and decorated in a childish hand, it sent chills up my spine. "WE ARE MRS. MORTON'S GARDEN." Mrs. Morton smiled the biggest smile I had ever seen, through tears that flowed silently. Happy tears, you know. She looked back at me, spread her arms wide and said, "See, I told you the truth. This is my garden."

We had quite an afternoon in that school gymnasium. A real gala event. Presentations and speeches. Songs and poems. I had learned a few things about Mrs. Morton on that bus ride over. And I learned a few more, watching her with those kids that afternoon. She was growing a garden alright, filled with the hopes and dreams she had had to work so hard to cultivate in herself after the war. It may take a village to raise a child, but I learned that day that it takes a Mrs. Morton to grow a garden.

Love Suffers Long

Connie Mae Inglis

Love is a choice
In the day
Chiseled with a phone call, hearing the fall
In the staccato, sleep-deprived voice,
A mallet of hacking rants.
Hearing the anxious voice
Of the roommate, pleading for freedom
And rescue from the stone madman
Inside his walls.
The way of my day
Shifts
To action.
Despite questions somber,
Love still arrives
As first responder. Love—
     is patient. Love is kind.

Love is a choice
In the week
Chiseled with a fear so unclear,
The driving force of mania,

The serpent speaks—
Leading him to the deep, to the
Cold, dark, forest where creatures creep.
Homeless, hungry,
Alone, but not, for we
Still seek
To find, and un-bind the lies that entwine.
So love responds
Again.
We throw out our lifeline. Love—
    is not easily angered. Love keeps no record of wrongs.

Lynn J. Simpson

"A bedrock of support. Love—
always protects, always trusts, always hopes, always perseveres."

Love is a choice
In the months
Chiseled with the glassy-eyed face that has replaced
Our son, my flesh, my blood,
Pacing the psych unit floor,
Gouging a focused path for the door for more
Self-medication;
His determination
Countered by our dedication
To seek expert intervention;
Carved out diagnoses
And med orders for disorders
While we
Provide, alongside
Offerings of fast-food and snacks
And books and smokes,
Anxiously inward
Yet hoping him forward,
As love prevails
In the gifting. Love—
    is not self-seeking. Love does not dishonour others.

Love is a choice
In the year
Chiseled with calendar dates and endless waits
Etching his course,
The indeterminate force;
Time ticking, and slipping
Away.
Sitting in offices,
Inpatient, out, without
Clear understanding but trusting

The system.
Doctors, pharmacists,
Government, Social workers all insist:
Don't resist
Proper paperwork,
For framing financial stability,
The ability to accept our
New life,
So love sustains
A bedrock of support. Love—
    always protects, always trusts, always hopes, always
    perseveres.

Love is a choice
In a lifetime
Chiseled by unseen, altered state, but lonely fate
Stagnates
In solid relationship
And love's powerful grip.
I give—we give
So when lifestorms whip, and wheel and deal
A dirty hand,
The one, our son,
Yet triumphs against the odd illness,
Statuesquely carved
To stand, grand,
For love overcomes
In the sacrifice. Love—
    never fails.

A Peace that Never Ends

Bobbi Junior

"Don't sing it. I'm warning you. Don't sing it out loud!"

Despite my appeal, the melody began in a soft hum. Just like on Name That Tune, it only took a few notes before my brain latched onto the song, like a baby to the breast.

"Stop!" I demanded.

"But it's such a cute song, Brian." She laughed. "We used to sing it all the way to school. Remember?"

"I do remember. That's why I don't want you to sing it now. I want to focus."

Totally ignoring me, off she went, words and all.

"This is the song that never ends, yes it goes on and on my friend" . . ."

I hadn't seen Annie for over a decade, not since grade school, and the fact that we'd both ended up in the same community college writing course had me wondering how the universe was choosing to line things up for me. Today was Now, with a capital N. Annie was part of the past.

I'd invested years, not to mention a whole whack of money, to escape that past. I sure didn't need her stealing what I'd worked so hard to achieve.

I'd totally reinvented myself from that kid I was in school. Two years of behaviour modification and emotional regulation therapy, and the resulting bank loans to cover it was evidence of that. It was worth it, though. I'd learned to be, well, maybe not

comfortable but accepting of the fact that I have OCD tenden-
cies. Not full-blown obsessive compulsive disorder, but "enough
to disrupt your happiness"—my counsellor's words, not mine.
My words were a bit more graphic, if you get my gist. Therapy
was an intense process, like scrubbing and then reformatting
a hard drive. I had to reject all my old coping mechanisms and
learn strategies to manage symptoms that had ruled me for years,
symptoms that had more free will than I'd ever had. In the past
month, looping on a single thought or phrase had re-entered the
picture, and I was working hard to keep it under control. But
here was Annie, this girl—well, woman now— totally undermin-
ing my efforts.

I wanted to smack her!

Not allowed, though. Men can't smack women, even when
they're asking for it.

My hands gripped the beat-up table where we sat working
on the assignment, there in the student lounge. I took a deep
breath. Concentrated on my aura. Visualized my place of peace,
but I couldn't block it.

"Some people started singing it, not knowing what it was
. . ." She'd lowered her voice, as though that would make a dif-
ference. Fat chance.

A curse caught in my throat. I clenched my teeth, locked
my eyes on the notebook in front of me. I tried to get back into
the assignment, but the words wouldn't string together to make
sense.

I glared at Annie over the tops of my glasses as she calmly
sat across from me, focused on her own notebook. She chewed
on her pen a moment, and then went back to writing.

She'd stopped her humming, but I hadn't stopped mine.

I had to get control. Biting back my anger I got up, went
to the hall, and strode back and forth, focusing my thoughts,
repeating my mantra and breathing. Inhale 2-3-4, exhale 5-6-7-
8-9. Inhale 2-3-4, exhale . . .

"What's up, Brian. Are you okay?"

"Ca-rikey!" My exhale exploded, not quite loud enough for her to hear. But then, what did I care? Maybe she needed to find out what a peace stealer she was.

"No. I'm not okay. You've totally blown my ability to focus, Annie. You know that?"

She looked contrite. I'll give her that. "Why? What did I do?"

"I asked you not to sing that blasted song."

"What song? Oh, you mean the . . ." she paused. "Uhh . . . Lamb Chop song?"

Humph. I guess she was listening. Maybe she just hadn't realized how critical this was to my peace.

I took a cleansing breath.

My therapist had said I ought to educate people about my condition, not hide it or be ashamed. So there in the corridor, I told Annie about going to counseling, being diagnosed with mild OCD. How I got caught up in repeating actions, or how a thought or phrase would get into my head and loop over and over and over, and I'd have to struggle to break free of it.

I told her how therapy was helping, how I'd found spirituality, learned about my aura, taught myself to be one with the universe, how I'd found my peace.

I watched her for any sign of ridicule, but she looked serious.

"How's it working?" she asked.

"How's what working?"

"Your peace in the universe?"

"Pretty good," I said, still kind of angry and a bit unsure about sharing all this private stuff. My therapist said to be honest, though, so I carried on. "Until someone like you comes along." I tried to keep the tone out of it but didn't do very well.

She leaned against the wall and held my gaze. She really seemed interested. "So your peace depends on your circumstances?" she asked.

"Well, yeah, to a degree. We're one with our environment, so what happens in the environment affects us. Do you have

Lynn J. Simpson

"I am a branch in the vine." She gave me a wink.
"Google it," she said, and was gone

peace?" Actually, she looked calm, and, well, yeah, peaceful. Just then I had a sudden recollection of her in grade school. She'd been a wild, hyper little girl, always moving, always talking, always getting into trouble. I'd forgotten that about Annie.

"Do I have peace?" she repeated. Her eyebrows peaked, and her whole face seemed to brighten. "Yeah, Brian. Yeah, I do. And it's not dependent on my environment, or my circumstances, either. And you, old friend, can't steal it, even if you try. Not unless I let you."

"Let me? I don't get it. You have that much control over your own peace that you can stop someone stealing it?"

"I do. If I remain in the vine, my peace remains as well."

"In the wine? You're a drinker?"

She laughed, a wonderfully engaging laugh. Not condescending at all.

"Vine, my friend. Vine. I remain in the vine."

I cocked my head, puckered my eyebrows.

She cocked her head and quirked the corner of her mouth. "I am a branch in the vine." She gave me a wink. "Google it," she said, and was gone.

John 15:5

Bobbi Junior lives and works in Alberta, Canada with her husband of 30+ years, near her two grown children. Recently retired, she continues to be active on the InScribe Executive (www.inscribe.org). Bobbi's passion is to use story to show how God brings value for our suffering. Through memoir, Bobbi explores caregiving, grief, disability, and other life experiences, sharing mistakes made and victories won. Visit Bobbi's blog at www.bobbijunior.com to download samples of her award winning publications: a chapter of *The Reluctant Caregiver,* or her short story, *Tell Me About Today.* Also available is the complete serialized version of her book, *When the Bough Breaks.*

Connie Mae Inglis has lived life to the full with her husband and three children, working in Southeast Asia as a Bible translator, literacy worker, and teacher. She is passionate about serving minority language groups, being a grandma, and dabbling in the creative arts—mainly painting and writing. She writes in many genres and is excited about her soon-to-be released first novel, *Rewriting Adam.* Her life experiences are a testament to God's goodness and love and she is thankful each morning for the gift of life. You can find her at: conniemaeinglis.ca

Jack Popjes and his wife, Jo, worked in Brazil for 24 years, completing the linguistic, literacy and Bible translation program among the Canela people in 1990. Jack served as president of Wycliffe Canada for six years and of Wycliffe Caribbean for three years. He served Wycliffe Associates as a speaker at 500 banquets and other events to raise funds for Bible translation. He has six published books of true-story-based articles and is completing the second volume of a four-volume autobiography. Jack and Jo have three married daughters and eight grandchildren ranging in age from 20 to 29.

Joy Bailey grew up on the Canadian prairies where rolling hills, just-mowed hay and the meadowlark's trill make her heart sing. She will always be a prairie girl at heart. What began in childhood as made-up stories to put herself to sleep at night, became creating stories and songs for her three daughters and, eventually, her grandchildren. As a gentle encourager, Joy fills her short stories, children's stories, poetry, and songs with warmth, whimsy, and wonder. She hosts Writers' Café in Edmonton, Alberta, where she lives with her husband, The Cowboy. Find her joy-infused view of the world at www.scrapsofjoy.com.

Katherine Kavanagh Hoffman began writing in childhood, and has continued to do so, in a variety of genres, ever since. Born in Montreal, Quebec, she currently resides in Edmonton, Alberta. She has a BAR (1981) from NABC, Edmonton, AB and an MCS (1990) from Regent College, Vancouver, BC. Besides writing, Kathy enjoys dabbling in all kinds of art, reading, and learning new things. Kathy is planning to launch a new blog, A Complicated Faith, in the near future. She has blogged in the past at This Life is an Adventure. You can find the old and the new at kgehca.blogspot.com.

Tina Markeli: Born in East Germany, Tina was five when her family moved to Canada. She started school in a one-room school house in Saskatchewan but the family soon moved to Vancouver. That's where she got to know God in a personal way. After graduation from BC Institute of Technology, she served in the laboratory of a small mission clinic in Haiti and met her husband. Together they worked in a southeast Asian country where they raised two daughters, taught in a Bible College, and mentored church planters. Helmut and Tina have retired in Edmonton, Alberta.

Lynn J. Simpson understands the need for creating spaces for rest, renewal, and transformation. She's rarely without her camera, capturing breathing spaces to share. She's published *Breathing Spaces: A 21-Day Journal of Rest, Reflection and Renewal* and *30-Day Journal of Thankfulness, Success & Joy,* and contributed to *Short and Sweet Too* (Grace Publishing, 2017).

Read Lynn's musings on faith, hope, and love on her blog (lynnjsimpson.com).